HighTide and Paul Jellis in association with The Marlowe
and The North Wall present

KANYE THE FIRST

A world premiere by Sam Steiner

A co-commission by HighTide and Paul Jellis

Kanye The First premiered at HighTide Festival Aldeburgh on 12 September 2017.
Kanye The First then transferred to The North Wall from 20–22 September, then
HighTide Festival Walthamstow from 26 September–7 October before transferring to
The Marlowe from 11–14 October in a production directed by Andrew Twyman,
Associate Director of HighTide.

Supported using public funding by
ARTS COUNCIL ENGLAND

The North Wall Arts Centre

THE MARLOWE

KANYE THE FIRST

HighTide and Paul Jellis in association with The Marlowe
and The North Wall present

ANNIE	Imogen Doel
MOTHER	Caroline Faber
ADAM	Daniel Francis-Swaby
EVE	Keziah Joseph

Director	Andrew Twyman
Designer	Camilla Clarke
Lighting Designer	Jai Morjaria
Sound Designer and Composer	Alexandra Faye Braithwaite
Dramaturg	Roy Alexander Weise
Consultant Dramaturg (The Marlowe)	James Baldwin
Casting Director	Louis Hammond CDG
Assistant Director	Monique Touko
Production Manager	Ben Karakashian
Stage Manager	Benjamin Luke
Associate Sound Designer	Annie May Fletcher
Costume Supervisor	Rike Zoellner

CAST

IMOGEN DOEL I ANNIE

Imogen most recently appeared in *Twelfth Night* (National Theatre).

Other theatre includes: *The Taming of the Shrew* (Shakespeare's Globe); *A Midsummer Night's Dream, Marat/Sade* (RSC); *The Importance of Being Earnest* (Vaudeville); *Serpent's Tooth* (Almeida); *In the Vale of Health* (Hampstead); *Narrative, The Get Out* (Royal Court); *The Seagull* (Gaiety, Dublin).

Television includes: *Resistance* (RTÉ); *Misfits* (E4).

CAROLINE FABER I MOTHER

Theatre includes: *My Mother Said I Never Should* (St James); *The Iliad* (Almeida); *Luna Gale* (Hampstead); *The Taming of the Shrew* (RSC); *King Lear* (Young Vic); *Romeo and Juliet, Paradise Lost* (Headlong).

Television includes: *EastEnders, Merlin* (BBC); *Berlin Station* (Paramount); *Dis/connected* (Shine Productions); *A Good Murder* (Sally Head Productions).

DANIEL FRANCIS-SWABY I ADAM

Daniel recently appeared in *Twelfth Night* (Royal Exchange).

Other theatre includes: *On Fleek* (Royal Court); *Les Blancs* (National Theatre); *Milk Milk Lemonade* (Ovalhouse).

KEZIAH JOSEPH I EVE

Theatre includes: *Silver Lining* (Rose, Kingston); *Wuthering Heights, Romeo and Juliet* and *Twelfth Night* (Royal Central School of Speech and Drama).

Radio includes: *Doctor Who, The Archers, Watership Down* (Radio 4).

CREATIVES

SAM STEINER | WRITER

Sam Steiner is a playwright and screenwriter from Manchester. Sam's debut play, the award-winning *Lemons Lemons Lemons Lemons Lemons*, was produced by Walrus Theatre (a company he co-founded). It has had three sell-out runs at the Edinburgh Fringe and toured nationally. The play has since been produced all over the world in several different languages. Other pieces of Sam's work have been showcased at the Royal Exchange, Soho Theatre, Southwark Playhouse, Sala Beckett in Barcelona and Cannes Film Festival. He has recently completed an attachment at Paines Plough as their Playwright Fellowship and holds an MA in Screenwriting from the National Film and Television School. Sam is also under commission at Paines Plough and Theatre Royal Plymouth.

ALEXANDRA FAYE BRAITHWAITE | SOUND DESIGNER AND COMPOSER

Alexandra Faye Braithwaite trained at LAMDA.

Recent and upcoming designs include: *Jam, A New Play for the General Election* (Finborough); *Room* (Theatre Royal Stratford East); *Rudolph* (West Yorkshire Playhouse); *The Remains of Maisie Duggan* (Abbey, Dublin); *Torch* (New Diorama); *Grumpy Old Women* (UK tour); *The Tempest* (Royal & Derngate); *Simon Slack* (Soho); *Diary of a Madman* (Gate/Traverse); *The Rolling Stone* (Orange Tree); *Happy to Help* (Park); *The Future* (The Yard); *My Beautiful Black Dog* (Southbank Centre); *Hamlet is Dead, No Gravity* (Arcola); *BUTTER* (The Vaults); *Juicy & Delicious* (Nuffield); *The Flannelettes* (King's Head); *Remote* (The Drum, Theatre Royal Plymouth); *His Dark Materials* (North Wall); *The Fastest Clock in the Universe, The Dreamer Examines His Pillow* (Old Red Lion); *XY* (Theatre503/ Pleasance, Edinburgh); *The Shelter* (Riverside Studios); *Project Strip* (Tara Arts); *Lonely Soldiers* (Arts); *Faustus* (The Old Laundry); *Blackout* (Castle).

As Associate: *The Glass Menagerie* (Nuffield); *Dracula the Musical* (Soho); *Secret Theatre* (UK tour); *Glitterland* (Lyric, Hammersmith); *Jumpers for Goalposts* (Watford Palace/Hull Truck).

CAMILLA CLARKE | DESIGNER

Camilla Clarke trained at the Royal Welsh College of Music and Drama, graduating in 2014 with a BA (Hons) in Theatre Design.

Recent designs include: *Frogman* (Curious Directive at the Traverse); *The Day After and Trial By Jury* (English National Opera); *No Place for a Woman* (Theatre503) and *Wind Resistance* (Royal Lyceum).

Other designs include: *Human Animals* (Royal Court) and *Seagulls* (Volcano Theatre).

Camilla was a winner of the Linbury Prize for Stage Design in 2015. Other Awards include the Lord Williams Prize for Design and The Prince of Wales Design Scholarship.

LOUIS HAMMOND cdg | CASTING DIRECTOR
For HighTide: *Heroine* (HighTide Festival/Theatr Clwyd);*The Sugar-Coated Bullets of the Bourgeoisie* (Arcola/HighTide Festival); *Harrogate* (HighTide Festival/Royal Court/House).

Theatre includes: *The 5 Plays Project, Creditors, The Member of the Wedding, Dirty Butterfly, The Indian Wants the Bronx* (Young Vic); *Inkheart, The Funfair, Romeo and Juliet* (HOME Manchester); *The Distance* (Sheffield Crucible/Orange Tree); *Romeo and Juliet* (Sheffield Crucible); *Primetime, Violence and Son, Who Cares, Fireworks* (Casting Associate at the Royal Court); *Amadeus* (Chichester Festival Theatre); *The Winter's Tale* (Regent's Park Open Air); *The History Boys* (Sheffield Crucible); *Driving Miss Daisy* (UK tour); *Batman Live* (world arena tour); *The Trial of Dennis the Menace* (Southbank Centre); *The Resistible Rise of Arturo Ui* (Liverpool Playhouse/Nottingham Playhouse); *Blue/Orange* (Arcola); *Von Ribbentrop's Watch* (UK tour); *Mrs Reynolds and the Ruffian, Brighton Beach Memoirs, Absent Friends* (Watford Palace); *All My Sons* (Curve, Leicester); 50th Anniversary Season of 50 Rehearsed Readings, Caryl Churchill Season, International Residencies and new writers' Rough Cuts presentations (Royal Court); *Loot* (Tricycle); *Blowing Whistles* (Leicester Square); *Testing the Echo* (Tricycle/Out of Joint tour); *The Importance of Being Earnest* (UK tour/ Vaudeville); *Donkeys' Years* (UK tour); *Rock'n'Roll* (Royal Court/Duke of York's); *Jus' Like That* (Garrick).

Louis was Head of Casting at *The Bill* (Thames TV), and also cast films *Arsene Lupin, Ne Quittez Pas, Beyond Re-Animator* and *Mirrormask.*

He is a member of the Casting Directors' Guild of Great Britain and Ireland.

BEN KARAKASHIAN | PRODUCTION MANAGER
Ben Karakashian graduated from Royal Holloway University of London with a BA Honors in Drama and Theatre Studies.

Production management credits include: *Unknown Island* (Gate); *These Trees are Made of Blood, Richard III, The Plague, New Nigerians, Kenny Morgan, The Divided Laing* (Arcola); *Working* (Southwark Playhouse); *Big Guns* (The Yard); *All Our Children* (Jermyn Street); *Acedian Pirates* (Theatre503); *Death Takes a Holiday, Ragtime, Titanic the Musical, In the Bar of a Tokyo Hotel, The Mikado* (Charing Cross); *Frontier Trilogy* (Rabenhof Theatre, Vienna); *Home Chat* (Finborough); *The Frontier Trilogy* (Edinburgh Fringe Festival); *The Man Who Shot Liberty Valance* (Park); *Our Ajax* (Southwark Playhouse); *The Bunker Trilogy* (Southwark Playhouse/Seoul Performing Arts Festival/Stratford Circus).

BEN LUKE | STAGE MANAGER
For HighTide: *The Sugar-Coated Bullets of the Bourgeoisie* (HighTide Festival/Arcola).

Other theatre includes: *The Snail and the Whale* (world tour); *The Hotel Cerise* (Theatre Royal Stratford East); *The Gruffalo* (West End/Broadway/world tour); *The Scar Test* (Soho); *Darknet* (Southwark Playhouse).

JAI MORJARIA | LIGHTING DESIGNER

Jai Morjaria trained at the Royal Academy of Dramatic Art (RADA) specialising in Lighting Design.

Theatre includes: *A Trip to the Moon* (Barbican Concert Hall); *No Dogs No Indians* (UK tour); *A Midsummer Night's Dream* (Southwark Playhouse); *Complicite Young Company* (Hackney Downs Studio); *A Village of Romeo and Juliet* (New Sussex Opera Company); *Breaking Up Is Hard to Do* (Upstairs at the Gatehouse); *Sister Act The Musical* (Alban Arena); *Trident Moon* (Finborough); *Acorn* (Courtyard); *Scrooge and the Seven Dwarves* (Theatre503); *Out There on Fried Meat Ridge Road* (White Bear/Trafalgar Studios 2); *The Beggar's Opera* (Jerwood Vanbrugh); *Royal Academy Opera Scenes* (Drill Hall Studios); *Macbeth* (Outdoor – Valley of the Rocks, Exeter).

Upcoming designs include: *The Cunning Little Vixen* (Arcola); *Alice In Wonderland* (Birmingham Old Rep); *The Importance of Being Earnest* (Outdoor – Valley of the Rocks, Exeter). Jai was the winner of the 2016 Association of Lighting Designer's ETC Award and has been nominated for an Off West End Award for Best Lighting Designer in 2016.

MONIQUE TOUKO | ASSISTANT DIRECTOR

Monique Touko is an emerging theatre director. Her training includes being a *Truth about Youth* associate at Ovalhouse Theatre and Observer Mondays at the Royal Exchange – which involved shadowing Ellen McDougall on *The Rolling Stone*. Her relationship with Royal Exchange cultivated in a three-month placement through the Regional Theatre Young Directors Scheme. This involved assisting Matthew Xia on *Wish List*, including its transfer to Royal Court and also assisting Emma Callander from Theatre Uncut on B!RTH festival.

She was selected to embark on the Introduction to Directing Course at the Young Vic, led by Sacha Wares and is receiving ongoing mentorship in-house. Her directing credits include *A Number, Animal Farm, Gourds* by Chino Odimba at Royal Exchange, and *The Sting* by Suzette Coon at Arcola Theatre.

Most recently she directed *See You At the End* by Alexis Boddy at Theatre503. Monique was an assistant director and administrator for ALT, which is an actors' training programme that targets BAME actors from low income backgrounds and provides an alternative to drama school resulting in an industry showcase. She is a freelance facilitator who has worked with Royal Exchange, Royal Court and The Challenge to provide workshops for young people, and received training from Company Three led by Ned Glasier. In addition, she is a script reader for Talawa Theatre Company and Bruntwood Prize.

ANDREW TWYMAN | DIRECTOR

Andrew Twyman is currently the Associate Director at HighTide Theatre and an Associate Artist at Live Theatre Newcastle.

For HighTide as Associate Director: *The Sugar-Coated Bullets of the Bourgeoisie* (Arcola).

For HighTide as Assistant Director: *Those Who Trespass* (ArtsEd); *Forget Me Not* (Bush).

Theatre includes: *Machinal* (ArtsEd); *Odd Shaped Balls* (Old Red Lion/Edinburgh Festival/Space UK); *Don't Smoke in Bed* (Finborough); *Te Karakia* (Vibrant 2015 at Finborough); *Reason and Force* (King's Head); *Fair Exchange* (Tabard).

Andrew was also a member of the writing programme at the Live Theatre, Newcastle.

H|GH
T|DE

A MAJOR PLATFORM
FOR NEW PLAYWRIGHTS

HighTide is a theatre company.

We produce new plays in an annual festival in
Aldeburgh (Suffolk) & Walthamstow (London) and on
tour.

Our programming influences the mainstream. Our
work takes place in the here and now.

HighTide: Adventurous theatre for adventurous people.

H|GH T|DE

2017

OVER A DECADE OF INFLUENCING THE MAINSTREAM

Our eleventh HighTide Festival premiered new works by Sam Steiner and Nessah Muthy as well as returning work from Theresa Ikoko.

All three productions featured at HighTide Festival, Aldeburgh before transferring to HighTide Festival, Walthamstow for the first time.

Nessah Muthy's debut production **Heroine,** transferred to Theatr Clwyd and Sherman Theatre following its premiere at HighTide Festival 2017.

Sam Steiner's **Kanye The First** transferred to North Wall Arts Centre and The Marlowe Theatre following its premiere at HighTide Festival 2017.

We were delighted to welcome back **Girls** by Theresa Ikoko after its successful debut in 2016. **Girls** opened as part of the British Council Showcase at the Edinburgh Fringe Festival 2017 before returning to HighTide Festival. Following HighTide Festival, the production transferred to Salisbury Playhouse and The Drum, Theatre Royal Plymouth.

For full details, visit hightide.org.uk

H|GH T|DE

WE NEED YOUR SUPPORT

There are very talented young playwrights in the UK, and if they are lucky they will find their way to the HighTide Festival Theatre season in Suffolk. I hope you will join me in supporting this remarkable and modest organisation. With your help HighTide can play an even more major role in the promoting of new writing in the UK.

- Lady Susie Sainsbury, Backstage Trust

HighTide is a registered charity and we could not champion the next generation of theatre artists and create world-class productions for you without ticket sales, fundraising, sponsorship and public investment.

To undertake our work this year we need to raise over £750,000.

We need your help to make these targets. You can show your support by: making a donation; buying Festival tickets; recommending the Festival to your friends; donating your time to help work on the Festival; writing to your local councillor and MPs about how much you value the HighTide Festival.

If you would like to discuss making a donation to HighTide, please speak to francesca@ hightide.org.uk or call on 0207 566 9765.

We are thankful to all of our supporters, without whom our work simply would not take place.

HighTide Theatre is a National Portfolio Organisation of the Arts Council England

Leading Partner: Lansons

Major Funder: Backstage Trust

Trusts and Foundations
Adnams Charitable Foundation; The Channel 4 Playwrights Scheme, The Carne Trust, The Eranda Rothschild Foundation, Garrick Charitable Trust, Harold Hyam Wingate Foundation, The John Thaw Foundation, The Martin Bowley Charitable Trust, The Noël Coward Foundation, Parham Trust, Peter Wolff Theatre Trust; Suffolk Community Foundation

Individual Supporters
Tim and Caroline Clark, Sam Fogg, Jan Hall, Diana Hiddleston, Tony Mackintosh and Criona Palmer, Clare Parsons and Tony Langham, Leah Schmidt, Mark and Deirdre Simpson, Lord and Lady Stevenson, Graham and Sue White.

Corporate Sponsors
Neil Ewen and all at Central Estates ActIV, The Agency, Central Estates Fullers, Lancasters' Home & Garden, United Agents.

PAUL JELLIS

Paul Jellis is an award-winning theatre and events producer. His work encompasses new writing, multidisciplinary performance, interactive theatre and immersive experiences. He has produced several productions for prestigious awards schemes, including the Leverhulme Bursary, JMK Award, JP Morgan Award and Kevin Spacey Foundation Artists of Choice, and his productions have won awards including Fringe Firsts, Musical Theatre Network Awards and Off West End Awards. His production of *Barbarians* at the Young Vic was nominated for an Olivier Award for Outstanding Achievement in an Affiliate Theatre.

As well as producing work under is own name, Paul is Creative Producer of the critically acclaimed interactive-theatre specialists Bad Physics, and was previously Executive Producer for the award-winning and internationally acclaimed new-writing company nabokov. In 2016 he was an inaugural member of The Old Vic 12, where he is currently Bicentenary Producer. He is also Festival Producer for HighTide.

Paul has produced and presented work at major theatres and festivals all over the UK and internationally including 59E59 Theaters New York, Jagriti Theatre Bangalore, National Theatre, Young Vic, Lyric Hammersmith, Soho Theatre, Bush Theatre, Gate Theatre, Sheffield Theatres, Bristol Old Vic, Birmingham Rep, Traverse Theatre and Manchester Royal Exchange. He has also developed and produced experiential events with global brands, including Ray-Ban, Courvoisier and PlayStation.

www.pauljellis.co.uk

The North Wall
Arts Centre

The North Wall is based on the campus of St Edward's School in Oxford. Built in 2007, the ground-breaking arts centre shares the school's mission to educate and inspire.

The North Wall exists to provide opportunities for artists, young people and its audience to make and experience art of the highest quality. Its vibrant theatre programme focuses on new writing and experimental work, offering a platform for early career artists as well as some of the UK's foremost touring companies, including Shared Experience, 1927, Out of Joint and ATC.

The North Wall is also home to ArtsLab, a programme of initiatives throughout the year that supports the production of new work and development opportunities for artists, including free residential projects for emerging artists aged 18–25. Since 2015, The North Wall has run TheatreCraft, an ArtsLab residency for new writing which offers emerging writers and directors to develop scripts under the guidance of industry mentors. The ArtsLab programme of home-grown artistic outputs also includes productions, co-productions and a range of participatory and educational initiatives for children, young people and the wider community.

The North Wall, South Parade, Oxford OX2 7JN
@thenorthwall
thenorthwall.com

THE MARLOWE

Creating experiences that enrich, inspire and entertain

The Marlowe is one of the country's most successful regional theatres, bringing the work of prestigious companies such as the National Theatre, Royal Shakespeare Company, Matthew Bourne and Glyndebourne Opera to audiences in Kent. The Marlowe are committed to nurturing and inspiring creative talent with new writing at the heart of what they do.

Roar, The Marlowe's new-writing development programme, works to support emerging writers and artists by providing the opportunity to develop bold and exciting new work through mentoring, workshops, funded research and development and work-in-progress sharings.

Since reopening in 2011, The Marlowe has been committed to championing new writing, and to date have been involved in the realisation of a number of productions including *Beached* by Melissa Bubnic, which premiered at The Marlowe Studio in 2014 before transferring to Soho Theatre, London. This was followed by *A Better Woman* by Simon Mendes De Costa in 2015. The Marlowe have also co-produced a number of new-writing productions, most recently *Box Clever* by Monsay Whitney, produced with nabokov, which premiered at the Paines Plough Roundabout at the 2017 Edinburgh Festival Fringe; *Run the Beast Down* by Titus Holder, which premiered at The Marlowe Studio before transferring to the Finborough Theatre, London, in January 2017, and *Warrior Poets*, which was developed in collaboration with Wise Words Festival and directed by Lemn Sissay, and premiered at The Marlowe Studio in October 2016. Other productions include *Mobile* with The Paper Birds Theatre Company and Edinburgh Fringe First Award-winning *Fabric*, in association with Robin Rayner and TREMers.

The Friars, Canterbury, CT1 2AS
info@marlowetheatre.com
marlowetheatre.com

This production was developed through The Marlowe's Roar programme, which was made possible with the support of The Marlowe Theatre Development Trust. Registered Charity no 1120751

KANYE THE FIRST

Sam Steiner

2

Thanks

To Paul Jellis and everyone at HighTide: Steven Atkinson, Francesca Clarke, Robyn Keynes, Holly White and Martha Rose Wilson. Thanks for thinking this was a good idea.

To our creative team: Camilla Clarke, Jai Morjaria, Alexandra Faye Braithwaite, Louis Hammond, Monique Touko, Ben Karakashian, Ben Luke and Luke Robson for their perceptiveness, depth of thought, and boundless talent.

To my dramaturgs, James Baldwin and Roy Alexander Weisse, who are both geniuses and fixed the play at least twice each.

To Imogen Doel, Caroline Faber, Daniel Francis-Swaby and Keziah Joseph for their fearlessness, compassion and dedication.

To Andrew Twyman for making this whole thing happen, pushing me to be bolder and having faith whenever it fell short. And for never letting me get away with anything.

To Marnie Podos and Scott Chaloff for their belief, encouragement and ambition.

To James Grieve, George Perrin, Jon and NoraLee Sedmak and everyone in the Paines Plough office for an inspiring and life-changing 9 months.

To Alistair McDowall and Simon Stephens for their galvanising teaching.

To Sarah Cullum, Emma Dewherst, Lanre Malalou, Eleanor Wright and everyone at The Marlowe who helped make our Roar development week happen. It was invaluable.

To George Attwell Gerhards and everyone around that Edinburgh table for the idea. And to all my friends that read drafts along the way.

To Rebecca Myers and Nicole Davis for their patience, support and vitamin-rich cooking.

To the Unwritten Dance Troupe for their creativity, friendship and good taste in all-too-often-forgotten mid-noughties pop bangers.

To my family for always getting excited.

To Charlotte Holtum for getting me through.

And to Kanye West, the greatest living rockstar on the planet.

S.S.

For Jiggy Steiner
The College Graduate

Roles

ANNIE
ADAM, *and others*
EVE, *and others*
MOTHER, *and others*

Note on Text

I think this play works best when the parts are played by actors
of the following ethnicities:

Annie – white
Adam (*etc*.) – black
Eve (*etc*.) – black
Mother – any

A forward slash (/) indicates the point of interruption in
overlapping dialogue.

A dash (–) indicates an interruption of speech or train of thought.

An ellipsis (…) indicates either a trailing, a breather or
a hesitation.

The lack of a full stop at the end of a line indicates a certain
pace or forward momentum.

Punctuation or lack thereof is written to suggest delivery rather
than to conform to the rules of grammar.

*This text went to press before the end of rehearsals and so may
differ slightly from the play as performed.*

The words 'THIS IS A TRUE STORY' appear for a moment then vanish.

ANNIE. Lucy!?

ADAM. What

ANNIE. You called me Lucy.

ADAM. Err no I didn't

ANNIE. Who the fuck is Lucy?

ADAM. I didn't… Who's Lucy? I don't know.

ANNIE. I'm Annie.

ADAM. I know. Annie. You're Annie. Let's just – let's go back to the talking thing.

ANNIE. Who's Lucy?

ADAM. nobody.

Pause.

Lucy's like my… she's this girl that's going out with my mate Chris.

ANNIE. Oh.

ADAM. I don't really know her.

ANNIE. Oh.

ADAM. She barely even speaks to me.

ANNIE. Right.

ADAM. So it's not a… like an issue or – don't read into it or whatever

ANNIE. Okay.

Sorry.

ADAM. No it's cool.

Pause.

ANNIE. Errr. Okay yeah let's just – get back to…

ADAM. Yeah?

ANNIE. Yeah. I've just like – I've wanted this for ages so…

ADAM. Okay. Yeah uh – yeah me too.

ANNIE. Okay um I'll go.

I wanna… errr… I wanna taste your cum in my mouth

ADAM. She's a country singer.

Beat.

ANNIE. What?

ADAM. Lucy. She err she sings these country songs. Like she's from… like she's from Tennessee or something? But she's not.

*

EVE. Annie.

ANNIE. I like your hat by the way.

EVE. What?

ANNIE. Your hat. It's nice.

EVE. It's a bit much / isn't it.

ANNIE. Kinda looks like a halo.

EVE. Really – like a / halo?

ANNIE. Angel's halo – saint's halo? – is it heavy?

EVE. Heavy?

ANNIE. Yeah heavy – like on your head does it feel heavy? Does your neck hurt or anything from the err from the weight?

EVE. You okay?

ANNIE. Yeah I just wanna start wearing hats.

EVE. You should.

ANNIE. I'd look great in hats.

EVE. I think you would.

ANNIE. You should get some wings. Complete the whole...

EVE. I'm – I'm gonna do that now, yes.

ANNIE. Some big fuck-off wings like a... *albatross*.

EVE. I'll look into it.

ANNIE. Cool

They smile.

You don't... so I had this um – the other day, I was in
a Starbucks

*

MOTHER. You had this look about you

ANNIE. Mmm.

MOTHER. Like you'd just seen some higher being. You looked
so happy. I kind of clapped my hands to my mouth at the
sight of you.

MOTHER claps her hands to her mouth.

ANNIE. Yeah.

MOTHER. And then obviously raced you to hospital.

ANNIE. But we / were

MOTHER. You'd perched her paws on your shoulders – one on
each shoulder and your heads were together.

ANNIE. Me and the Labrador.

MOTHER. Yeah. And you couldn't really breathe. You weren't
breathing. I listened for your breathing but there was just
this raspy sound that I'm pretty sure was your windpipe
closing up?

ANNIE. Shit.

MOTHER. You were that obsessed with this animal.

ANNIE. It's funny cos I like – I remember it really vividly but my memory totally airbrushes the bit where I can't breathe

MOTHER. That's funny.

ANNIE. Yeah. In my head it's just this perfect... moment

MOTHER. Why did you ask me about that?

*

EVE. A Starbucks?

ANNIE. I was in a Starbucks and you know how they write your name on the cups now? Like they take your order and then they write your name on your to-go coffee cup? It's a pretty smart marketing strategy. But, so the other day the guy asked me my name and I told him it was Cunt. Like I just said 'Oh my name is Cunt.' He was like 'What?' and I just said 'yeah it's Cunt – C-U-N-T, Cunt. That's my name.'

EVE. Right.

ANNIE. And he got all awkward and said his pen had run out but then this woman next to me turned to me, looked me up and down, and said: 'You're a monster.'

EVE. Whoa.

ANNIE. I know!

EVE. Bitch.

ANNIE. Right?

EVE. That's so judgemental.

ANNIE. I know. And her baby was so ugly as well.

They laugh.

But you don't... like...

EVE. What?

ANNIE. Think I'm...

EVE. What – No!

ANNIE. Okay cool.

EVE. You're taking care of Mum and stuff.

ANNIE. Yeah no I know. I knew that.

EVE. How is she?

ANNIE. Who?

EVE. Mum.

ANNIE. Oh. Yeah she's okay. I mean she's in pain.

EVE. Yeah.

ANNIE. Can't get the smell of piss out of my hands.

EVE. I just think that's in your head.

ANNIE. Yeah.

EVE. She won't let me help.

ANNIE. Yeah.

EVE. I tried

ANNIE. I know.

EVE. But you're hinting / I can tell

ANNIE. I'm not hinting. Wasn't / hinting

EVE. She won't let me

ANNIE. Mmmm.

EVE. I don't get it.

    She's so... formal. I don't get it. Treats me like I'm not a real
    person.

ANNIE. You're...

EVE. What?

ANNIE. She doesn't want your hands covered in her piss.

    Pause.

EVE. I walked in the other day and she like... did her hair?

*

ANNIE *is removing* MOTHER*'s pants*.

MOTHER. Is there blood?

> *Pause.*

> Is there blood?

ANNIE. Some, yeah.

> *Silence.*

MOTHER. Thank you.

> *Beat.*

ANNIE. No.

> You saved *me* so…

> *Beat.*

MOTHER. Did I?

ANNIE. Yeah. From my stupid allergies. / The… dog

MOTHER. Oh yeah – yeah.

*

The scenes begin to merge into a cacophony. From now,
ANNIE*'s dialogue is directed to* ADAM *unless stated otherwise.*

ADAM. Sorry this is / fucking stupid

ANNIE. What does she look like?

ADAM. What?

ANNIE. Lucy. The country singer. What does she look like?

ADAM. … She's got dark hair?

MOTHER. It was funny. That day.

ADAM. And brown eyes.

ANNIE. Okay

MOTHER. Cos it was probably the closest you've come to death.

ADAM. And she's got this uh these, like, I think you call them dimples?

EVE. I heard her run into her room and start doing it

ADAM. You know those kinda folds of skin that you get in cheeks?

MOTHER. But I remember feeling so in awe of you.

ADAM. Sorry.

EVE. and I just waited in the hall for five minutes. And it was – when I spoke to her – Mum – when she got out and we spoke – I could tell she was in loads of pain but she wouldn't show it? She was just smiling with her teeth all clenched? And it was obviously hurting her even more to hide it so I just like – I just faked a phone call and said I had to leave.

I wanted to ask / you –	ADAM. Can you just forget I / said anything

ANNIE. What if you imagined I'm her.

ADAM. What?

EVE. Annie?

ANNIE. Like if you look at me and imagine that my hair is dark like hers and my eyes are brown and my cheeks have dimples in them.

EVE. Do you / um...

ADAM. That's weird

ANNIE. Just – come on – just – yeah – it's fucking easy

ADAM. Errr

ANNIE. Do it – I want you to.

   Beat.

   Okay?

ADAM. Yeah.

   Beat.

ANNIE. Yeah? That's – I'm her now right? In your eyes.

EVE. Do you / um...

ADAM. She doesn't speak like that.

ANNIE. How does she speak?

ADAM. She's Irish.

ANNIE. Seriously?

ADAM. Yeah.

ANNIE. Okay. Errr. (*Hammy Irish accent.*) My name's Lucy.
My – my – my name's Lucy and I'm from...

Pause.

ADAM. Oh uh... Limerick.

ANNIE (*Irish accent*). My name's Lucy and I'm from
Limerick.

Laughs.

What do you wanna say to me, Adam?

ADAM. Hi Lucy

ANNIE. Hi Adam.

Pause.

ADAM. It's weird seeing you without Chris.

ANNIE. I don't want to talk about Chris.

ADAM. What do you want to talk about?

ANNIE. Look at me like I'm her.

He does.

ADAM. Okay.

ANNIE. I want to talk about me.

ADAM. Okay... I um I think you're beautiful?

ANNIE. Yeah?

ADAM. Yeah. I've thought that for ages. I wanted to tell you.

ANNIE. Why didn't you?

ADAM. I couldn't. Because of Chris.

ANNIE. I don't want to talk about Chris.

ADAM. Sorry.

ANNIE. Tell me again.

ADAM. I think you're beautiful. I think you're the most beautiful person ever.

ANNIE. Thank you.

ADAM. I think you're like *TV* beautiful

ANNIE. Touch me.

ADAM. Okay.

ANNIE. I want you, Adam.

ADAM. Okay… Just there?

ANNIE. Yeah.

ADAM. Ah

ANNIE. Ah

Pause.

ADAM. I love you Lucy.

ANNIE. Ah.

ADAM. Ah.

ANNIE. Say it again.

Suddenly the whole world shakes.

Argh

ADAM. You're checking your

ANNIE. Yeah

ADAM. Can we – can you just check after?

ANNIE. I need to.

ADAM. Why?

Beat.

…why?

ANNIE. My mum's ill – I need to –

ADAM. oh / shit

ANNIE. Where the fuck's my phone

ADAM. I'm… sorry about –

ANNIE. Don't be – it's really fucking inconvenient.

Oh.

ADAM. What?

ANNIE. It's just a news bulletin.

ADAM. Okay. Uh can we…

ANNIE. Kanye West died.

ADAM. Oh. How?

ANNIE. You look just like my dad.

ADAM. What.

*

EVE. Do you remember Mark? The guy I used to – my ex. With like – the moustache and the neck tattoo?

ANNIE. Err yeah?

EVE. He messaged me the other day.

He's going through this crappy time – his dad's disabled and they're about to get evicted or something so he's um desperate and like / threatening to…

ANNIE. Trying to get back in there?

EVE. Uh… yeah.

ANNIE. That's hard.

EVE. Yeah.

Yeah. He's just a piece of shit.

Pause.

ANNIE. Feel like I never see you any more.

EVE. Me too.

It's good that we... like I always feel like I know what you're up to so...

ANNIE. Yeah.

ANNIE smiles at her, sadly.

EVE moves into position for the next scene. ANNIE remains in this one for a moment, looking at EVE.

*

HELEN *is played by the actress playing* EVE. EXEC *is played by the actor playing* ADAM.

HELEN. Thanks for seeing us.

EXEC. Thanks for coming in.

ANNIE. I'm Annie and this is Helen.

EXEC. Great to meet you. I'm   HELEN. Such a pleasure to be
Will. I'm acting head of   here.
sales here.

ANNIE. You actually look really like my dad.

EXEC. Errr okay / great   HELEN. ERRRR so

ANNIE. Sorry that's weird – ignore me.

*

MOTHER. How's Eve?

ANNIE. yeah she's okayish

MOTHER. How did she look?

ANNIE. She's got this horrible hat

MOTHER. Oh really?

ANNIE. Yeah it's the worst thing I've ever seen…

*

HELEN. What we'd offer your company is a / different approach.

ANNIE. A different viewpoint on / these transactions.

HELEN. Essentially we see each transaction as an individual point of climax in a long-gestating interpersonal relationship.

ANNIE. Gestating, / yeah.

HELEN. Each transaction is actually the culmination of a drawn-out chain of events / that have

ANNIE. What's making me choose your face cream over someone else's face creams? What's making me choose your face cream over a banana or a Twix or a pack of strawberry laces or / a new pair of… sorry yeah.

HELEN. So we're all well-versed in the idea that selling is about creating a need. If I want to sell you a pen I'm going to tell you something that you absolutely *need* to write down and then ask you to buy a pen from me in order to do so. Our firm is suggesting a reconfiguration of this idea entirely. /

At this point the following scene begins over the top of HELEN*'s monologue.*

If transactions are viewed as the climax points in an ongoing interpersonal relationship, the need that we are aiming to create isn't a need for face cream, it's a need to access that point of climax, it's a need for proof of the connection you feel. It's a need, essentially, to feel demonstrably worthy of love. If we can endow your brand with enough character, with enough personality, enough warmth, we believe your customers will want to come back time and time again. They will actively look forward to the purchase rather than associating it with the guilt we usually feel when spending money. Essentially we're talking about shifting their emotional experience of consumption from a place of guilt to a place of love.

*

MOTHER. She sent me this really funny video the other day. It was of this hamster doing

MOTHER *descends into laughs.*

he just keeps doing these

MOTHER *descends into laughs.* ANNIE *waits patiently.*

Backflips. He keeps doing these backflips. Over the edge of his little pen thing.

MOTHER *descends into laughs. She hoots and coughs and splutters.*

Did you see it?

ANNIE. Yeah. It is good.

MOTHER. I loved it!

ANNIE. Yeah, it is undeniably good. I think I'm gonna go to bed.

MOTHER. Okay.

ANNIE. Yeah. You're okay to…

MOTHER. Yeah I'm fine. I'm good.

ANNIE. Don't need any help…

MOTHER. No.

ANNIE. Great.

Silence. ANNIE *hesitates.*

MOTHER. Are you… waiting for something?

ANNIE. No I'm… I don't know what I'm waiting for.

*

ANNIE *sits alone watching footage of a hamster doing backflip after backflip over the edge of its pen. This should be projected onto an enormous screen so that the hamster looks a lot bigger than* ANNIE's *tiny, curled-up form.*

The video loops and starts again.

This should go on for a long time after it stops being funny.

Silence.

Maybe a sudden white light shines on ANNIE *for a fraction of a second?*

*

MOTHER *screams.*

ANNIE *runs down the stairs.*

ANNIE. alright alright you're okay. Okay. Just, okay squeeze my hand

> *Grabs hand.* MOTHER *looks at* ANNIE *and screams even more.*

MOTHER. WHO ARE YOU

ANNIE. Mum it's me. Here – wriggle out of your – yep

> MOTHER *pushes* ANNIE *away.*

Mum

MOTHER. Who the fuck are you get away from me.

> MOTHER *screams.*

ANNIE. Mum you've pissed yourself. You've fucking pissed yourself and / you need me to clear it up

MOTHER. Why are you calling me that

ANNIE. We've done this – this is what we do / – okay just

MOTHER. GET OUT OF MY HOUSE GET OUT OF MY HOUSE

ANNIE. Please don't get all Alzheimer's on me as well

> EVE *enters.*

EVE. Whoa who are you?

ANNIE. Evie

EVE (*calling upstairs*). ANNIE!

ANNIE. Hey dickhead it's me.

EVE. Mum who is this?

ANNIE. Eve.

MOTHER. I don't know he just showed up. He keeps calling me Mum. He tried to take off my trousers.

EVE. Get the fuck away from her! ANNIE! Mum where's Annie?

ANNIE. Whoa. Evie. It's me.   MOTHER. She's asleep. She
                                                                        was / in bed

EVE. Where is she – what have you done with her? What have you

> EVE *attacks* ANNIE. *It should feel aggressive and dangerous, not staged.*

done –

with –

her

> ANNIE *pushes back.* EVE *falls to the floor.* EVE *looks up at* ANNIE, *terrified. She tries to get in between* ANNIE *and* MOTHER.

ANNIE. What the fuck are you doing?

EVE. Where is she? Mum where

MOTHER. WHAT HAVE YOU DONE WITH MY DAUGHTER

EVE. Mum get the phone.

ANNIE. Guys. It's me. It's Annie. Are you both – Is this some joke I'm / not in on

> EVE *grabs some kind of weapon.*

EVE (*to* MOTHER). Call the police.

ANNIE. You trying to kill me?

EVE. IF YOU COME A STEP CLOSER

ANNIE (*roaring*). IT'S ME LOOK AT ME

   Pause. EVE *looks at* ANNIE, *wide-eyed*.

EVE. Are you…

ANNIE. Yes. Jesus Christ.

EVE. You're…

ANNIE. Look like you've just seen a ghost.

EVE. I mean you can't be…

ANNIE. I'm your fucking sister you lunatic.

EVE. You look just like him.

ANNIE. Who? Dad?

EVE. You *sound* like him.

ANNIE. I don't.

MOTHER. Evie, who are you talking about?

ANNIE. She's saying I look like Dad. I'm nothing like him.

EVE. Kanye West.

   Pause.

ANNIE. What?

*

ANNIE. We were supposed to be at football. This was like two
   weeks after Dad had 'gone on holiday'. And we were sitting
   waiting for training to start when the guy in the bar pulled
   down the big projector screen and put the news on and, you
   know, we saw the towers burning – with all the smoke pouring
   out of them and stuff. You were almost definitely wearing
   that old, baggy Arsenal shirt with Bergkamp on the back. And
   I was probably wearing that Nike sweatband round my head
   because it always made me feel pretty kung fu. But then
   someone – the reception guy with the mohican? – he came and
   told us that football training had been cancelled. And we
   thought, we assumed it was cos Graham, our coach, was *in*
   9/11. Like he was in the towers and he was dying. And you

started crying but I just kind of froze. Cos the night before –
I hated Graham, he always made me collect up all the cones –
and the night before I'd like wished that he died. Yeah I'd
wished he was dead and so I thought – in that moment – that
I had... somehow... *caused* 9/11. That it was my fault the
planes had... Just like um... And you were screaming like:
'*he's in the towers, he's on fire*' and I was just paralysed with
guilt and – and then well...

You're not gonna...? Okay.

The reception guy saw you crying and had a panic that we
were too young to know about terrorists and stuff so he took
us to the kids' club booth and put a VHS on – a recording an
old episode of that – what's-his-name's – interview show?

EVE. Michael Parkinson.

ANNIE. Yes!

MOTHER. Don't help him.

EVE. Sorry – got too wrapped up in the story.

ANNIE. Yeah Parkinson so we sat round watching long-form
celebrity interviews in this little kids' club booth – kids' club
booth with like a ball pit and a swan – like a swan-shaped ball
pit yeah – while outside everyone was shouting and scared and
angry and then I thought I heard his voice from outside. Dad's.
I thought I heard him shouting for us. Shouting for *me*. Asking
if I was okay. Telling me that it wasn't my fault at all and that
Graham just had a cold or something. But it wasn't Dad's
voice at all. It was just someone that sounded like him.
Looked like him. And he wasn't saying that. He was just
ordering coffee. So I just sat there watching the Michael
Parkinson show feeling guilty and scared and sad about Dad
and responsible for *everything* so...

Is that enough detail for you?

Pause.

Fucking hell. Okay right err – you have a mole on your left
shoulderblade and you climbed Kilimanjaro two months ago

and claim to have had some crazy, pure, silent epiphany
moment at the top.

EVE. Hadn't told / Mum about that.

ANNIE. And Mum Mum… errr okay – when you were
seventeen you travelled like three hundred miles on your own
to see the Talking Heads and they didn't play 'Psycho Killer'.

Pause.

MOTHER. How do you know all of this?

ANNIE. Cos I'm me.

EVE. This is kind of a lot for us to take in.

Silence.

ANNIE. so… so when you look at me – now – when you're
looking at me right now, you don't see me. The real me.
You see…

Pause.

EVE. A um… a forty-year-old black man with a goatee.

ANNIE. And my voice, it doesn't sound like my voice?

EVE. Annie's voice.

ANNIE. Yeah.

MOTHER. No.

EVE. It sounds… Chicagoan.

MOTHER. Chicagan?

EVE. American.

MOTHER. Definitely American.

Silence.

MOTHER *moans in pain. She wets herself.*

ANNIE *instinctively goes over to her to help.*

No.

ANNIE. Mum.

Pause.

MOTHER. I um… I know it's you. I can tell. I couldn't before. But now I… I can – I can feel it I promise – But… I can't let you

ANNIE. Why?

MOTHER. It's disgusting.

Pause.

EVE. I'll do it.

EVE slowly takes off MOTHER*'s pants and gets her some new ones.* ANNIE *watches in silence.*

*

NEWSREADER (*either onstage or pre-recorded video/audio*) *is played by the actor playing* ADAM.

ANNIE *stares into a mirror.*

She runs her fingers through her hair.

She pulls at the skin around her eyes.

The sound of a phone ringing.

NEWSREADER. A man bearing a startling resemblance to recently deceased hip-hop star Kanye West has been spotted outside an office block in Central London. A /

ANNIE. Hello?

A woman's heavy-breathing, performed (*either on- or offstage*) *by the actress playing* EVE.

Hello? Is anyone…

The line goes dead.

*

EXORCIST *is played by the actor playing* ADAM.
EXORCIST *is a consummate professional not a spooky witch doctor.* ANNIE *is hiding her face using a hat and a hood.*

ANNIE. Thanks for seeing me so quickly.

EXORCIST. I had a cancellation.

ANNIE. Oh really?

EXORCIST. Yep.

ANNIE. Why did they cancel?

EXORCIST. They didn't say.

ANNIE. Oh.

EXORCIST. I assume they had a conflicting engagement.

ANNIE. Yeah.

EXORCIST. That's usually why people cancel things.

ANNIE. Yeah.

EXORCIST. I don't actually like discussing other / clients'

ANNIE. Oh you've got a confidentiality / kinda

EXORCIST. Well

ANNIE. Exorcist–client privilege

EXORCIST. Something like that

ANNIE. Cool.

    Pause.

EXORCIST. If you'd like to take your hood and your hat off / for me.

ANNIE. You look like my dad.

EXORCIST. Uh.

ANNIE. He's a spy. So I guess you guys are in quite different fields.

    That's probably inappropriate for me to say.

EXORCIST. I understand that first consultations can seem scary. Especially for people from communities such as our own.

ANNIE. What do you mean 'communities such as' –

EXORCIST. There's a certain stigma / around

ANNIE. like we're not from the same…

EXORCIST. Well my family are actually from Brooklyn. I just grew up here.

ANNIE. Mine aren't.

EXORCIST. You know what I mean.

ANNIE. I'm not black.

EXORCIST. Err okay.

ANNIE. African American. AfricanAmericanBritish. Sorry.

EXORCIST. No it's fine.

ANNIE. I'm white and I'm from here – London.

EXORCIST. Right.

ANNIE. Not that I'm *at all* – like I'd be perfectly happy if I *was* black, African A– yeah. But I'm not.

EXORCIST. Okay.

ANNIE. Like sometimes I wish I was. Cos you guys are better at sports and at singing, dancing. And I'm not good at any of those things.

EXORCIST. We're getting off-topic.

ANNIE. Smarter. I think. As well. Like fuck I wish Obama was British am I right?

EXORCIST. Yeah he's actually kind of a problematic figure.

ANNIE. But I'm just not black – that's not who I am.

Argh you think I'm crazy.

EXORCIST. No.

ANNIE. I'm really not. I'm actually someone that would
normally think this kind of stuff – possession – is complete
bullshit.

EXORCIST. Lots of people do.

ANNIE. Like I'm very much a member of the educated liberal
elite.

EXORCIST. Right.

ANNIE. Sorry.

EXORCIST. Don't worry.

Pause.

ANNIE. The hat and the hood?

EXORCIST. Yeah.

Pause.

ANNIE. Okay.

Pause.

EXORCIST. Okay. Well first, this is fairly unprofessional of
me, but first I should say that I'm really happy you're alive

ANNIE. No

EXORCIST. And I'm a big fan of your music. Particularly the
later albums.

My brother got kind of alienated after *808s* but I keep telling him that's when you really started digging into things.	ANNIE. No I'm – No

ANNIE. I'm not Kanye.

EXORCIST. Errr

ANNIE. My name's Annie.

EXORCIST. Okay.

ANNIE. My family don't recognise me. My work, my friends don't… They all think I'm him.

EXORCIST. So you think

ANNIE. I'm not even that in to his music.

EXORCIST. You think *he* has, in some way, taken over your physical form.

ANNIE. Yeah.

EXORCIST. Kanye West

ANNIE. Yeah. Cos I think I'm still me. I don't feel any different. When I look in the mirror it's still me. My hair and skin colour / and

EXORCIST. But to everyone else

ANNIE. Apparently

EXORCIST. Right.

Pause.

ANNIE. Can you help?

Pause.

EXORCIST. Tell me about yourself.

ANNIE. What – just…?

EXORCIST. Tell me about Annie.

ANNIE. Uh okay. I'm twenty-seven. I work in PR. I grew up in North London. Went to uni here and now work… Thinking of moving down to Peckham but… Errr I've got a sister. Younger sister. Called Eve. Evie.

EXORCIST. So you're not an only child.

ANNIE. Uh. No?

EXORCIST. Interesting.

ANNIE. Why?

EXORCIST. Well Kanye is an only child.

ANNIE. Right.

EXORCIST. Tell me about your relationship with her.

ANNIE. Evie? What d'ya wanna know? Her favourite fucking movie or something?

EXORCIST. Whatever you want to tell me.

ANNIE. *Pinocchio* – that's her favourite movie.

EXORCIST. Okay.

ANNIE. Um we get on well, yeah. She's kind of like a perfect person.

EXORCIST. What makes you say that?

ANNIE. Well so she's three years younger than me but she did all of the stuff way before I did. Booze and sex and stuff.

EXORCIST. Okay.

ANNIE. And she's crazy smart too, it's not like she's a fucking dropout. She's doing this – wants to do this PhD on like 'the inherent violence of narrative form'.

EXORCIST. Sorry a / dropout?

ANNIE. She got the idea when she was – she went up Kilimanjaro – literally scaled a mountain on the other side of the world – and apparently at the top she had this uh… don't know why I'm telling you this but uh… she was the first of her group to get to the top and she had this moment where she looked out over everything and everyone was still scrambling up the last climb but it felt – to her – it felt like there was just *her* – in the world – for that, you know, for a few seconds and she was just up there – alone – above everything – just checking it out. I'm wittering.

EXORCIST. Sounds wonderful. / But

ANNIE. Yeah.

EXORCIST. Why would you think I'd assume she's a dropout?

ANNIE. Oh errr – I wouldn't – didn't. Just wanted to clarify.

EXORCIST. It's just interesting to me that you'd use that word.

ANNIE. Why?

EXORCIST. Well Kanye West's first album was called *The College Dropout* and there is a widely held understanding that a lot of his work is based on the tensions between society's, in particular his academic mother's, expectations of him and the scale of his own personal ambition.

ANNIE. Oh.

EXORCIST. Yeah.

ANNIE. Are you…? Are you like *showing off*? Cos I'm not… Like I need your help, I'm here cos I *need* you.

EXORCIST. Yes, of course.

ANNIE. I'm not Kanye West.

EXORCIST. Of course.

ANNIE. Good.

EXORCIST. Do you love her? Annie's sister.

ANNIE. Yeah. She's amazing.

EXORCIST. Okay.

ANNIE. Why did you say 'Annie's sister'? That's me. That's my sister.

EXORCIST. Sure.

ANNIE. Why are you talking about me in the third person?

EXORCIST. I want to remain clear.

ANNIE. You don't think I'm Annie.

EXORCIST. I do.

ANNIE. You're being suspicious.

EXORCIST. I believe that you think you're her.

ANNIE. What does that mean?

EXORCIST. Well, there has never been a proven instance of possession leading to bodily transfiguration. This isn't Harry Potter.

ANNIE. Harry / Potter

EXORCIST. I personally don't believe it's possible.

ANNIE. What are you saying?

EXORCIST. Well, Mr West, I think it's much more likely that the spirit of this girl, Annie, has taken over control of your body.

ANNIE. What?

EXORCIST. That she is speaking through you and controlling your actions.

ANNIE. You're kidding.

EXORCIST. That would make much more sense to me.

ANNIE. Wouldn't I be like… aware of that?

EXORCIST. Not always. Sometimes we like to forget the means we take to gain power.

ANNIE. I haven't / 'gained power'.

EXORCIST. I think I can get her out of you, sir. It's actually quite a simple / procedure.

ANNIE. I'M NOT HIM.

EXORCIST. Kanye?

ANNIE. Stop it.

EXORCIST. Can I call you Kanye?

ANNIE. My name's Annie.

EXORCIST*'s voice begins to digitise, glitch and pan around the room.*

KANYE THE FIRST   33

EXORCIST. It would be an honour.

I'm a huge fan. I love your work.

It means so much to me.

'Runaway' changed my life.

ANNIE. Stop…

Stop

Stop it

*

A synth pad appears in the centre of the stage. ANNIE *is drawn towards it.*

She presses a button. It makes a sound. The world shakes.

She presses another one. A vocal sample of her mother's scream.

Another – a female sex moan.

Another – a long beep.

Another – her mother's voice.

MOTHER. It's – It's – It's – It's strange. Not to know

Another – EVE's voice.

EVE. Enough – Enough – Enough for for for you

These become chopped together and begin to work without ANNIE *– who steps away.*

Another – a man's voice.

MAN. The things things things she does with her mouth.

Another – a child's voice:

CHILD. Daddy? Can I sing you a song? One of One of One of yours

Can I?

This is chopped together with other vocal samples and maybe a beat? But it should not last long.

The voice of the child begins to sing the old gospel song 'I'll Fly Away'. ANNIE *remixes it as she goes.*

*

ANNIE *wears her hood and hat, covering up her face.* NURSE *is played by the same actress that plays* EVE.

ANNIE. Excuse me?

Nurse?

Hi errr we've been waiting for an hour / and

NURSE. We'll get to you as soon as we can

ANNIE. Yep but the people you just called arrived after us

NURSE. They had an appointment

ANNIE. We have an appointment

MOTHER. Annie, it's fine.

ANNIE. We had an appointment an hour ago

NURSE. Well we're very understaffed.

ANNIE. Well my mum's in pain so

NURSE (*looking at* MOTHER *bemusedly*). Your… mum?

ANNIE (*intensely*). Yes.

NURSE. Everyone here is in pain

ANNIE. I know that but

NURSE. Everyone has to wait their turn

ANNIE. She's sitting there clenching her bladder like mad just so she doesn't piss herself / in public.

NURSE. Okay I need you to calm down, sir.

ANNIE. Don't call me sir – I'm not a sir – What – you gonna make me tell the kids' club story again?

NURSE. Err excuse me?

MOTHER. Annie just sit down.

Pause.

ANNIE. Sorry.

NURSE. We'll get to you as soon as possible.

Pause. MOTHER *winces in pain.* ANNIE *puts a hand on her back.*

MOTHER. It's okay. There's a lot of people here.

ANNIE. We got here before them.

MOTHER. Maybe it's more complicated than that. Maybe it's a really complex system.

ANNIE. It's not a complex system. They're just like – looking at you and deciding what they think they know about what you're going through.

MOTHER. But maybe it is though. Don't they have a traffic-light code or something? A ranking system. Yes. They must do. To do with how much pain everyone's in? I'm sure some of these people are in really horrible amounts of / pain.

Suddenly ANNIE *stands. Takes off hood and hat.*

ANNIE. I'm Kanye West.

Pause.

I'm Kanye West. I'm alive. I'm here.

*

ANNIE. Can I get you like a cup of tea or something?

MANAGER. Tea?

ANNIE. Yeah.

MANAGER (*amused*). Err yeah?

ANNIE. What uh – how do you… take it?

MANAGER. Do you have mint tea?

ANNIE. I don't know. I can check.

MANAGER. Loose-leaf if possible.

ANNIE. I don't think we have loose-leaf.

MANAGER. That's okay. I'm enjoying the novelty anyway.

ANNIE. Novelty?

MANAGER. You offering me tea.

He starts laughing heartily.

ANNIE. There's no mint.

MANAGER. Oh fuck. Fuck. Fuck. Fuck. You asshole. You big dripping shitty asshole. What the fuck do you think you're doing not having loose-leaf mint tea when I get to your fucking house in fucking Britain after you're fucking resurrected you fucking piece-of-shit animal.

Pause.

He suddenly starts laughing.

Laugh with me, man.

ANNIE *forces herself to laugh.* MANAGER *laughs too.*

This place is adorable by the way

ANNIE. This is weird for me.

MANAGER. It's weird for me. I cried at your funeral. Kim gave this speech, man. Shivers. Like get that girl into fucking Congress. The fucking UN need some of that shit. Michelle – nothing, boring, dull, ugly, past it. KK baby! KK!

ANNIE. I think we need to clear something up.

MANAGER. Mh-mm?

ANNIE. I'm not him. I just – my mum's ill. Needs help. And that – me looking like... – I thought that could help her.

MANAGER. So you've just commandeered his body

ANNIE. *Commandeered?* / No.

MANAGER. And used it for your own personal gain.

ANNIE. Whoa, I'm helping my / *sick mum*

MANAGER. I'm playing with you! When did you get so serious?

ANNIE. I'm actually not a very serious person.

Beat.

MANAGER. Look, I don't care. Whether you're him or
you're... Gandhi – whoever. It's cool.

ANNIE. 'It's cool'?

MANAGER. Yeah. It doesn't matter to me at all. Have you got
any grapes?

ANNIE. Um. No.

MANAGER. I'm really in the mood for some grapes.

Beat.

ANNIE. You look kinda like my dad.

MANAGER. Poor fuck.

ANNIE. He's an astronaut.

MANAGER. Cool!

ANNIE. Yeah. It's pretty cool.

MANAGER. You want kids?

Pause. ANNIE *eyes him.*

ANNIE. Err. Wow. Dunno.

Not for ages.

I'd wanna like...

I'd just wanna bring them up in the right environment.

MANAGER. LA's a pretty nice environment.

ANNIE. Yeah.

I dunno.

That's not really what I mean.

Pause.

Anyway I feel like I've only just got my vagina looking how I'd like it to look so I don't wanna – you know – shove another life-form through it too soon.

MANAGER *laughs.*

Sorry. That's… not appropriate.

MANAGER. When did you learn sarcasm?

ANNIE. When I grew up in Britain.

MANAGER. I like it.

Beat. ANNIE *smiles.*

The sound of a phone ringing.

ANNIE. Sorry can I just…

MANAGER. Of course.

ANNIE. Hello?

A woman's heavy-breathing, performed (either on- or offstage) by the actress playing EVE.

Who is this?

The actress of EVE *whispers: 'Kanye?' in an American accent.*

ANNIE *groans, ends the phone call and turns back to* MANAGER.

Sorry.

MANAGER. No. It's sweet about your mom.

ANNIE. Yeah. She's a deeply incapable person so…

Beat.

What do you want from me?

Beat.

MANAGER. I just want you to be yourself.

*

The lights are blinding ANNIE.

INTERVIEWER *is played by the actress playing* MOTHER.

INTERVIEWER. Tell me, slowly, what you believe to have happened.

ANNIE. When?

INTERVIEWER. Well, when you 'woke up'.

ANNIE. Uh. Okay. So I heard my mum screaming.

INTERVIEWER. Your mother?

Beat. ANNIE *eyes* INTERVIEWER.

ANNIE. Yes.

INTERVIEWER. That's fascinating.

ANNIE. Why?

INTERVIEWER. Well your mother is obviously no longer with us.

ANNIE. Yes she is. With us.

INTERVIEWER. Oh… in *here*? (*Points to* ANNIE*'s heart.*)

ANNIE. No. Alive. On Earth. Just… keeping on keeping on.

INTERVIEWER. Okay.

ANNIE. Sorry.

INTERVIEWER. Why are you sorry?

ANNIE. When I'm nervous I just spout shit. Fuck I shouldn't swear.

INTERVIEWER. It's okay.

ANNIE. My mum says it's the curse of my generation.

INTERVIEWER. What is?

ANNIE. That we uh… sorry this is boring.

INTERVIEWER. No, go on.

ANNIE. Um. Okay. She says that you lot, your… your age bracket, your social imperative – that's the phrase she uses – your social imperative was to have something to say. She said she'd spend days just sitting there, trying to think of something to say. Something she could slip into different conversations. Some idea or some point about the world that would make her sound smart – intelligent. Cos she – her brain works quite slowly – she's a bit up in the clouds.

INTERVIEWER. Okay.

ANNIE. Sometimes.

INTERVIEWER. And your / generation.

ANNIE. But my generation, our social imperative is just: keep talking. Just: fill the silence.

INTERVIEWER. Is this something your mum taught her students?

Pause.

ANNIE. Well she teaches seven-year-olds so… she tried to keep it all a bit chirpier than that.

INTERVIEWER. Your mother, Donda West, taught English Literature at Chicago State University.

Pause.

ANNIE. That's not my mum.

INTERVIEWER. Okay. So tell me who it is that you think you are.

Pause.

ANNIE. I'm…

Pause.

I guess I'm not really sure.

INTERVIEWER. Have recent events made you feel, in any way, validated?

ANNIE. 'Validated'?

INTERVIEWER. Yes.

ANNIE. Uh I don't really know what you mean.

INTERVIEWER. Well you wrote and released a song called 'I Am A God'

ANNIE. I didn't

INTERVIEWER. Okay

ANNIE. Stop saying… I hate the way you say 'Okay'. Every conversation we've had since

INTERVIEWER. What do you mean *we've* had

ANNIE. Like I'm dangerous… like I'm some volatile substance

INTERVIEWER. Okay.

ANNIE. Like I'm about to explode.

INTERVIEWER. So you're not about to explode?

ANNIE. No?

INTERVIEWER. Great.

ANNIE. Yeah.

INTERVIEWER. Do you feel validated?

ANNIE. I don't know what you mean, Mum.

INTERVIEWER. Mum?

ANNIE. Sorry.

INTERVIEWER. Do you think you're a god?

ANNIE. No.

INTERVIEWER. Okay.

ANNIE. As in what?

INTERVIEWER. As in a… higher being.

ANNIE. A higher being?

INTERVIEWER. Yes.

ANNIE. No.

INTERVIEWER. No.

ANNIE. I mean I guess everyone feels like that sometimes right?

Sometimes it feels like everyone else in the world is just a variation on a theme.

INTERVIEWER. Okay.

ANNIE. Stop it.

Pause.

INTERVIEWER. Have you been in touch with your kids yet?

ANNIE. What?

INTERVIEWER. Your wife, Kim Kardashian has so far denied your identity.

ANNIE. Yeah.

INTERVIEWER. But I was wondering if you'd spoken to your kids. North is four and Saint is one?

ANNIE. Um…?

INTERVIEWER. Great ages.

ANNIE. Okay?

INTERVIEWER. You haven't spoken to them.

ANNIE. No.

INTERVIEWER. Did you enjoy being a parent?

Pause.

ANNIE. Yeah. I did.

INTERVIEWER. That's nice.

ANNIE. I wanna talk to you about parenting actually.

INTERVIEWER. Okay.

ANNIE. So errr I had this teacher at uni.

INTERVIEWER. Didn't you drop out of uni?

ANNIE. Before I dropped out.

INTERVIEWER. Okay.

ANNIE. And she had this thing about pushing her students.

INTERVIEWER. Right.

ANNIE. She'd never let them get away with a seven or an eight out of ten. She wouldn't stop until they got to like a twelve right?

INTERVIEWER. Okay.

ANNIE. And she, one time after the lecture, she wanted to give me some advice right? She said Annie – Kanye – she said: so many students don't give everything they've got in them. They don't become everything that they could be. And do you know why?

INTERVIEWER. Why?

ANNIE. This is what she said to me.

INTERVIEWER. Okay.

ANNIE. She said: the problem is that as soon as they do anything good – in the world – when they're like two or three – their parents start clapping right. They put their hands together and they just start clapping,

ANNIE *starts clapping*.

congratulating them like: 'well done, well done, you're amazing.' Then she looked me dead in the eye and she said: Ann-Kanye – Don't clap.

INTERVIEWER. 'Don't clap'?

ANNIE. Don't clap.

INTERVIEWER. Wow.

Pause.

ANNIE. Yeah.

INTERVIEWER. I'd say that's pretty cruel.

ANNIE. Do you have kids?

INTERVIEWER. I do.

ANNIE. Are they happy?

Pause.

*

KIM KARDASHIAN *is played by the actress that plays* EVE. KIM *carries her two children in her arms. They should be played/signified by something abstract – not real children.* ANNIE *is initially distracted by some task or screen.*

KIM. Baby.

ANNIE. *Baby?*

KIM. It's me baby.

ANNIE. Evie, what are you doing?

KIM. Who's Evie, baby? It's me. You recognise me, baby. You do. You recognise your kids.

Beat.

ANNIE. Kim?

KIM. Yeah.

ANNIE. Kim.

KIM. Yeah baby.

ANNIE. Fuck it's really

KIM. Yeah

ANNIE. You

KIM. Yeah

ANNIE. Off the telly.

KIM. I'm sorry I didn't come earlier.

ANNIE. No, it's…

KIM. I didn't believe it.

ANNIE. Yeah me neither.

KIM. It hurt too much.

ANNIE. Sure.

KIM. I was so confused. I was so totally confused. But now it all makes sense.

ANNIE. *Does* it?

KIM. Of course you're here.

   Of course you're not gone.

   You could never be gone.

   I'm sorry, baby.

   I just… sorry I thought I had this whole speech down and now it's – I'm forgetting it – now that you're in front of me.

ANNIE. Uh it's okay.

   Kim Kardashian.

KIM. Sorry they're actually really heavy now. Can you take North?

   KIM *offers one of the 'children' to* ANNIE. ANNIE *takes it. Holds it awkwardly. Stares down at it. Maybe the child starts crying and* ANNIE *has to bob up and down a bit?*

   I know I said some really horrible things to you.

ANNIE. Uh listen Kim – Miss Kardashian

KIM. I know I told you that you put yourself first before me and the kids

ANNIE. No / just

KIM. That I didn't like the version of you that you were becoming

But I'm looking at you now

And you're *so* real

It's the man I married

The father of my kids

And I thought I was never going to see *that* person again.

And I hated myself for ever trying to make *that* person into a different person.

I hated myself, Kanye. I promise I did.

I must look so ugly right now.

I bet my face looks disgusting.

I'm gonna turn around.

KIM *turns around.*

Pause.

Kanye?

ANNIE. I don't think I'm who you want me to be.

KIM. That's okay. That's okay. I know things will have changed. That's okay too.

I just don't want you to feel like you ever have to be a certain way for me?

I'm yours no matter what.

Pause.

ANNIE. You don't look like you do on TV.

KIM *turns around.*

KIM. I can change. I can – I have before – / I just want this to work –

ANNIE. No no it's – you look…

KIM. I just want us to be a happy family again.

ANNIE. you look like a goddess.

I've never seen anything…

The way your… hair does…

Pause.

ANNIE *brings herself back down to earth.*

I'm so sorry. I'm just totally not your husband. I know it looks like… And I know you must be having a shit time right now – I know you must be in pain and grief and – but this isn't… like these aren't my kids. This is all just a big – metaphysical… fuck-up. I'm sorry.

KIM *tries to stop herself crying – it's real, not fake.*

*

EVE *and* MARK (*who has a neck tattoo*). ANNIE *walks in on them.*

ANNIE. Oh.

EVE (*to herself*). Oh no.

ANNIE. Hi. (*Determinedly checking it's her.*) *Evie.*

EVE. Hey.

ANNIE. So /

EVE. Errr

Annie this is…

this is my friend Mark.

ANNIE. The one with the moustache and the neck tattoo.

EVE. Yep.

MARK. I shaved that off a while ago. Realised I looked like a right dick.

ANNIE. Ha.

MARK. Don't think we've met.

ANNIE. We have, I've just put on a lot of weight recently so you probably don't recognise me.

MARK. I do recognise you.

ANNIE. Right yeah.

Beat.

| I like your | EVE. Mark was | MARK. I should |
| tattoo. | just leaving | go. |

Awkward beat.

MARK. Thanks. It's dumb really.

ANNIE. It's like a cobra or…?

MARK. Rattlesnake.

ANNIE. Oh cool.

MARK. It's stupid.

EVE. Yeah.

MARK. I got it when I was eighteen and trying to be this big, threatening, super-intimidating guy.

ANNIE. Pretty lame, Mark.

MARK. And it doesn't come off even though I like… (*To* EVE.) don't wanna be that way any more.

Cos it's a tattoo so…

Beat.

ANNIE. Yeah. If you got like a talented designer on board you could probably make it look like a very interesting penis.

MARK *laughs briefly then it dies down.*

Sorry, it feels like I've walked in / on…

EVE. No no no.   MARK. no it's…

We were just catching up.

Mark's helping me
with work.

MARK. Yeah we've had some good discussions.

EVE (*jumping in*). Have you spoken to my mum?

Beat. Flicker of annoyance over ANNIE's *face.*

ANNIE. What?

EVE. They're operating.

Beat. ANNIE *looks at* MARK. MARK *looks down, guiltily.*

ANNIE. When?

EVE. She didn't tell you?

ANNIE. Haven't seen her

MARK. I'm gonna go.

EVE. Bye.

ANNIE. Bye.

MARK (*to* EVE). Listen, I'm um…

I'm sorry about your mum. That's shit.

EVE. Yeah.

MARK. But it doesn't… / change…

EVE. See you later.

He nods at ANNIE *and goes.*

ANNIE. What's going on? When's Mum's op?

EVE *closes here eyes and breathes in and out deeply –
calming herself down.*

Evie.

EVE. Why did you come here?

ANNIE. . . . I was gonna ask if you'd watched my interview

*

FAN *is played by the actor that plays* ADAM.

FAN. Do you want me to take my clothes off now?

ANNIE. Not yet.

FAN. Okay.

ANNIE. Listen we've gotta keep it down – my mum's in the other room.

FAN. What?

ANNIE. . . . I'm kidding?

FAN. Is your dad gonna come in and tell us we're doing something unholy?

ANNIE. My dad's dead.

FAN. Is he?

ANNIE. Yeah.

   He was a firefighter. He died saving a load of orphans.

FAN. Wasn't he a member of the Black Panthers?

ANNIE. Yeah that too.

FAN. Wow.

ANNIE. You look a bit like him.

FAN. What?

ANNIE. Never mind.

   Pause.

FAN. So why d'ya bring me back, Kanye?

   Beat.

ANNIE. I needed to blow off some steam.

FAN. I didn't even believe you were real till you came up to me at the bar.

ANNIE. Nobody seems to believe it at the moment.

FAN. You know what – fuck the naysayers, man.

ANNIE. 'God doesn't look like you.'

Maybe 'God doesn't look like you' is graffitied onto the stage.

FAN. Scum.

ANNIE. Yeah.

FAN. You don't care what they think.

ANNIE. Yeah.

FAN. When you went on TV after Katrina happened and said 'George Bush doesn't care about black people' you / didn't care

ANNIE. Stop.

Pause. They eye each other.

FAN. You're married.

ANNIE. I'm not married.

FAN. To a woman.

ANNIE. I'm not.

FAN. But you do wanna fuck me right? That's why you brought me here. I won't tell anyone.

ANNIE *laughs*.

What?

ANNIE. Normally guys talk about fucking *me*.

FAN. Oh well I can do that too.

Beat.

ANNIE. I'll think about it.

FAN. Okay. Or I could just sort you out?

ANNIE. You want to?

FAN. Yeah. Yeah I really want to. I really fucking want to.

ANNIE. What's your name?

FAN. Taylor.

ANNIE. Taylor. Sorting me out.

FAN. Can I…

> ANNIE *nods. Pause.*

ANNIE. It might not work. I haven't tried.

FAN. Okay.

> *Pause.*

> Whoa

ANNIE. What? Is it not there? Is there nothing there?

FAN. Oh my god.

> ANNIE *backs away.*

ANNIE. What's wrong?

FAN. What – no – god no – nothing's wrong – it's just – that's the most beautiful penis I've ever seen.

ANNIE. Really?

FAN. Yeah. It's like… stunning. It's… It's glowing

ANNIE. Glowing?

FAN. Yeah it's

ANNIE. What does it look like?

FAN. It's like… a work of art.

ANNIE. A work of art

FAN. Like a Renaissance painting. It's like… Mozart…

ANNIE. Are you okay?

FAN. I'm just a bit overwhelmed.

   Kanye West.

   Kanye West.

   I fucking love you man.

   Your music kinda saved my life – did I tell you that?

   You made me feel like… less alone.

   I thought we'd lost you but now *this*.

   Maybe ANNIE*'s crotch begins to glow?*

ANNIE. Are you… crying?

FAN. I just love you so much.

   Pause.

ANNIE. Put it in your mouth.

                              *

ANNIE *stares into the distance smoking a post-coital cigarette.*

A moment.

MANAGER *enters eating grapes.*

MANAGER. I think you can.

ANNIE. Yeah?

MANAGER. I think you can

ANNIE. I don't know anything about it.

MANAGER. You're a young, British white person. You've
   been to a hip-hop gig.

ANNIE. I've been but I've never – It wouldn't be disrespectful?

MANAGER. You *want* to.

ANNIE. No.

MANAGER. You do.

ANNIE. My mum could do with the money but

MANAGER. Did you go out the other night?

ANNIE.…No.

Pause. MANAGER *grins at* ANNIE. ANNIE *looks away.*

MANAGER. How would it be disrespectful?

ANNIE. Well it's not my place is it?

MANAGER. Why not?

ANNIE. To rap his songs. That's like… problematic. That's…
appropriation.

MANAGER. Why?

ANNIE. Cos like hip hop is for people from certain, you know,
certain backgrounds isn't it? Like poor backgrounds.

MANAGER. Kanye is middle class.

ANNIE. You know what I mean. Rapping is – that's – that was
a way for young people of a certain social – you know –
situation to to to tell *their* stories and I'd be taking advantage
of that wouldn't I? I'd be imposing myself on *Kanye's*
stories. I'd be hijacking / Kanye's –

MANAGER. Oh I see what's going on. You're putting your
nice little white middle-class box on hip hop and saying this
is just a way for poor black people to talk about gangs.
You're saying hip hop isn't an art form like novels or
paintings / or plays.

ANNIE. No I don't wanna do that at all.

MANAGER. Good.

ANNIE. But isn't there… isn't it different because the people
doing the hip hop are a – um – a traditionally – historically
even – historically, systematically oppressed group.

MANAGER. Well shouldn't hip hop be bringing us together not
tearing us further apart?

ANNIE. Um.

MANAGER. Do you wanna live in a multicultural society?

ANNIE. Obviously, yes.

MANAGER. Well I have always found that a properly integrated multicultural society relies on the free exchange of ideas and traditions between different ethnic and cultural groups.

ANNIE. Err yeah – yeah that sounds – exchanging stuff freely – that sounds good but

MANAGER. Well why are you putting a lid on that you fascist fuck?

ANNIE. Whoa, okay.

MANAGER. You fucking right-wing censorship machine. How goddamn dare you. You pig. You white-supremacist, Nazi cocksucker. I have a good mind to carve a swastika into your black forehead for those comments.

Beat.

ANNIE. Are you done?

MANAGER. Can I tell you the truth?

ANNIE. Yes please do that.

MANAGER. Nobody cares.

ANNIE.… What?

MANAGER. Nobody gives a shit.

ANNIE. It really feels like they might.

MANAGER. Nobody cares. As long as they get to sing along to the chorus of 'Gold Digger' – nobody cares.

ANNIE. Ha.

MANAGER. I swear to God.

Pause.

Look. People have hard lives, the world's a piece of shit, et cetera. And your music, *Kanye*, your music gives them some minuscule, momentary relief from that onslaught of pain and loneliness and guilt and shame and death and if you walk out on that stage and shout – (*Recites the first two lines of the chorus of 'Gold Digger'.*) for one tiny moment that voice in the back of their head goes quiet and they feel worthy and connected and adored.

And they will look up at you and they will love you like a god. Whether the fuck you are one or not.

Because it will *feel* real.

Baby.

Beat.

ANNIE. You are *so* American.

MANAGER. I'm just telling you what you want to hear.

ANNIE....okay?

MANAGER. You told me you'd wanted this for ages.

ANNIE. Did I?

                              *

ANNIE. Do you think…

EVE. What?

ANNIE. No, nothing.

EVE. Okay.

ANNIE. It's just…

EVE. What?

ANNIE. Nothing.

EVE. I need to talk to you about something.

ANNIE. It looks darker.

EVE. What does?

ANNIE. I swear it looks darker.

EVE. What looks darker?

ANNIE. My face.

EVE. Your face?

ANNIE. My skin yeah. It looks darker than it used to. I swear.

EVE. Well, yeah.

ANNIE. And I'm not tanned. I haven't been getting any sun.

EVE. Yeah.

ANNIE. It's just darker.

EVE. Yeah.

ANNIE. Where does Mum keep the photo albums?

EVE. I digitised them all for her.

ANNIE. Oh really?

EVE. Annie, can I talk to you about something?

World-shaking boot-up sound.

Remember Mark.

ANNIE. No – who's Mark?

EVE. The one with the neck tattoo.

Images of ANNIE *as a baby appear.* ANNIE *stares at them.*

What are you doing?

ANNIE. Do you think I've always looked a bit like Kanye West?

EVE. Uh.

ANNIE. Like here – I do look a bit like him don't I?

EVE. No.

ANNIE. No I know. But there's something. There *is* something.
Maybe it's my ears?

And my name right.

EVE. Your name.

ANNIE. Annie.

EVE. What about it?

ANNIE. Annie. Annie-ay. An-i-yay. An-ye. K-an-ye.

EVE. Sound like you're having a stroke.

ANNIE. Kan-ye. Kan-ye.

EVE. What are you saying? That you've always been Kanye?

ANNIE. No. Obviously not. That's stupid. But...

She keeps flicking through baby photos.

Her with ice cream on her face.

A load of her and her sister watching Disney's Pinocchio *on VHS.*

Maybe I was always meant to like... *become* him.

EVE. What?

ANNIE. Like eventually.

EVE. Become him?

ANNIE. Like before then, before I *became* him my life had no direction or story / or

EVE. Annie.

ANNIE. Mm-hm?

EVE. Mark has a tape of me.

Doing stuff.

And he's gonna

It's gonna be online.

Pause.

ANNIE. What are you doing?

EVE. I'm doing stuff to him. He's doing stuff to me.

ANNIE. What stuff?

EVE. Stop it.

ANNIE. What stuff?

Silence.

Maybe you'll be an internet star.

Like Kim Kardashian. Her sex tape's how she got famous isn't it?

Maybe like – strangers will watch it – you – and wank off to it.

Maybe people you know.

Maybe everyone you know.

Maybe Mum will watch it.

Maybe Dad will watch it.

And he won't even recognise you and he'll just be wanking off to / his own daughter

EVE. Stop it.

ANNIE. *You* made a sex tape.

EVE. Yeah.

Horrible silence.

ANNIE. Sorry.

I don't know why I said that.

I'm sorry.

Evie I'm sorry.

I was just fucking around. I'm sorry.

Please.

ANNIE *goes to hug* EVE. EVE *struggles initially, pushing her away, but then gives in.*

They stand there, hugging in silence.

EVE. This is more comforting now you're a big middle-aged man.

A beat and then they break apart.

Pause.

i don't know what to do.

ANNIE. Does he like… want something? or is he just gonna put / it up

EVE. He wants some money.

ANNIE. How much money?

EVE. Well now he wants a lot. Because of…

She nods at ANNIE. *Beat.*

ANNIE. I can get a lot of money.

EVE. Seriously?

ANNIE. Yeah.

Can we just forget I said that stuff?

Pause. EVE *nods.*

EVE. Thank you.

ANNIE. You're welcome.

Beat.

EVE. Why are you looking at me like that?

*

ANNIE. How are you feeling?

MOTHER. Perfect.

ANNIE smiles.

I'm fine.

ANNIE. That's good.

Pause.

I'm sorry I haven't been here much.

MOTHER. That's okay. I know you've got a lot on your mind.

ANNIE. Evie's been helping?

MOTHER. Yeah she has.

ANNIE. Great. And the private doctors? Really nice right?

MOTHER. Yeah – swanky. My doctor – it's funny – he looks a bit like David Byrne from Talking Heads.

ANNIE. That's great.

MOTHER. I was thinking how funny it'd be if David Byrne had decided to retrain as an oncologist in his sixties. I think that'd be so funny but also kind of make sense?

ANNIE. You've been pissing yourself less?

Pause. MOTHER *smiles, doesn't respond.*

Sorry.

MOTHER. Don't worry.

ANNIE. I didn't mean to make fun of you or…

MOTHER. Yes, well…

Pause.

ANNIE. Do you let Evie change you now?

MOTHER. Annie.

ANNIE. Do you?

MOTHER. No. I can change myself.

ANNIE. Okay. Cool. It doesn't hurt any more then?

MOTHER. Not really.

ANNIE. What's the doctor saying?

MOTHER. Says I'm on the up.

ANNIE. Oh really?

MOTHER. Yeah.

ANNIE. Cool.

MOTHER. Yeah.

Beat.

I watched your interview.

ANNIE. That's nice.

MOTHER. Thought you did well.

ANNIE. Interviewer went hard on me.

MOTHER. Do you think?

ANNIE. Yeah. I do.

MOTHER. I thought she was very fair.

ANNIE. I saw Evie digitised the photo albums.

MOTHER. Oh yeah.

ANNIE. That's cool.

MOTHER. Yeah it's great actually. It's really handy.

ANNIE. Do you think I used to look like him?

MOTHER. Who? Your dad?

ANNIE. Kanye West.

MOTHER. Oh.

ANNIE. In the photos.

MOTHER. I don't think so.

ANNIE. When I was born.

MOTHER. No. Definitely not.

ANNIE. So it's something that's happened since then.

MOTHER. Well…

ANNIE. Nurture.

MOTHER. Okay?

Beat.

I had this dream last night that I filled a whole bathtub with my own wee. That it kept coming and coming until it was spilling over the edges but I wasn't... it's not like real life where it's painful and embarrassing. There was bits of blood in it but that was fine – it just added a bit of colour. I kind of swam in it. In this bath of my own warm wee.

Very strange dream.

Pause.

Are you okay?

ANNIE. Yeah. I'm good actually.

MOTHER. Great.

ANNIE. Yeah.

MOTHER. That's lovely to hear.

ANNIE. I've got a manager now.

MOTHER. Wow!

ANNIE. Yeah it's exciting right?

MOTHER. I'm so happy for you.

ANNIE. Thanks. I mean, I'm doing it all for you and Evie so...

MOTHER. For our sins.

Pause.

I knew you could do it.

ANNIE. Do what?

MOTHER. Just achieve things I guess.

ANNIE. Right.

MOTHER. I don't want us to argue.

Pause.

ANNIE. It just never feels – when you say that – you always sound like you're speaking to a dog: 'Go get that ball! Go jump through this hoop! Yes! I knew you could do it!'

MOTHER. I'm sorry that you / think that.

ANNIE. I guess it just sounds fake.

MOTHER. Fake?

ANNIE. Yeah like you're off thinking about other things but feel like you should be encouraging.

MOTHER. It's not fake.

ANNIE. Okay.

MOTHER. It's the opposite of fake.

ANNIE. Yeah. Cool.

    Argh I turn into such a teenager when I'm with you.

    Pause.

    During which KIM *comes on stage with the kids. But* MOTHER *doesn't see them.*

    KIM *gets the kids ready for a family photo. Silently. Dreamily.*

    The kids are now represented by something slightly more tangible – maybe mannequins wearing the clothes?

    ANNIE *looks up at* KIM *and the kids but speaks to* MOTHER.

    I'm playing a gig

MOTHER. As him?

ANNIE. Well as me.

MOTHER. But you're doing his songs.

ANNIE. Yeah.

MOTHER. Do you know them?

ANNIE. I'm learning.

MOTHER. What name's on the ticket?

ANNIE. Well each person has their own name on their ticket – that's how ticketing works.

MOTHER. No I mean what name's at the top of the ticket?

ANNIE. Oh uh…

his…

His name.

MOTHER. Oh.

Pause.

ANNIE. All he did was steal bits out of old soul songs and put drums over them.

MOTHER. I don't want us to argue.

ANNIE. Can you just let me have this?

MOTHER. Let you have what? Let you lie and steal this man's life?

ANNIE. I know it's not – I know I'm not how you wanted me to turn out.

I know this isn't what you pictured.

But can you just let me have it okay?

Pause.

MOTHER. I can try. If you want me to. I can try.

ANNIE. I want you to.

MOTHER. Then I'm trying.

Pause.

ANNIE. I'm him, Mum. When people look at me that's who they see. That's the truth. That's what matters.

Pause.

Listen to me, Mum.

MOTHER. I have been listening to you, Annie.

ANNIE. I'm Kanye West.

*

Roars of a crowd.

A microphone stands at the front of the stage.

ANNIE *comes on stage.*

The roars sound louder, deafening.

The opening of Kanye West's 'Jesus Walks' plays over the speakers.

That moody, gospel beat.

It loops.

ANNIE *paces at the back of the stage like a predator stalking its prey.*

The spoken-word intro plays.

The choir sing the eponymous line: 'Jesus Walks'.

ANNIE *steps up to the microphone.*

*

MOTHER *stands at the microphone.*

Maybe at some point she takes it off the stand and sits on the edge of the stage, speaking into it.

A long beep runs throughout the scene.

MOTHER. It's strange. Not to know. For it to be happening. And for you not to know that it's happening. For you to be completely unaware. Maybe it's always like that. Maybe you're never – at that moment – at that exact moment – maybe you're never completely in-the-know.

It's funny.

It's funny.

There's this *man*... Don't laugh.

Chuckles to herself.

He um... he was a trainee teacher that I worked with when I... I must've been twenty-seven, twenty-eight. I'd just had Evie.

Annie was three? Maybe? Tony was still around then.
Although he was difficult obviously – just so constantly
restless. I think I was in Year 3 at the time which was always
my favourite – it was the one I really properly cracked I think.
Where I could really make the kids' eyes light up. But this guy
was a hopeless teacher. Bless him he was absolute car crash of
teacher. Watching his lessons was like watching a train
derailing in slow motion. All the people inside the train
screaming for their lives.

She does an imitation of someone screaming for their life.

She cackles with laughter.

His poor face. But he was a nice boy. Well-intentioned. He
drove me home once when my car was in for repairs and
when he dropped me off he waited until I was in the house to
drive away. Like he wanted to make sure I got in safely. And
I've always been shit at finding my keys so it must've been
minutes. I remember him telling me in the car about how he
sometimes poses for life drawing. As a nude model. Which
I thought was funny.

Well he got in contact with me on Facebook a few weeks
ago. He added me as a friend.

She beams at the audience.

It's so dark in here. I can't see anyone. Can we turn the
lights on?

The house lights come on.

That's nicer, I think.

So he works with guide dogs now. Animals. I think that's
much more appropriate. And he's still doing the nude
modelling. He loves it apparently. But he uh... I'd been
teasing him about how terrible a teacher he was and he
offered to cook me dinner as an apology – to make up for
me having to train such a headcase. He made seafood paella.
I KNOW! And then well, one thing led to another and just as
we got up to his bedroom he turns to me and he's sometimes
got this very earnest, straightforward way of talking that

doesn't – you know sometimes that can feel false I think –
but his doesn't, his just feels comfortable. Comfortable is the
right word I think. But he looks me in the eye and he just
says: 'Jenny, I should tell you – I'm absolutely awful at it.'

She laughs.

He says: 'I have never given a woman an orgasm and, trust
me, that is *not* for want of trying.' And I told him there was
a chance, a small chance that I might wee in the middle and
scream in excruciating pain. And he nodded and said that
seemed fair.

She laughs.

And guys. He was not wrong. It was SO BAD. SO BAD.
Elbows… *Knees…*

Shivers, jokily.

I just burst out giggling halfway through and he went bright
red and put his head in my chest and his arms around me.
And we just sat there for a while. Waiting for it to be okay
again. And I remember the rain being really loud outside the
window.

I didn't tell Annie about it. Or Eve. They don't know about
it. They're in the dark. Just like I'm in the dark now. We've
always been very open about that kind of thing. But I just…
I just didn't want them to know. And yet I'm telling you. I
think that makes me a terrible mother. I think I just wanted it
to be a main story in my life, not a supporting story in theirs.

I wish they'd listen to each other a bit more. They can be so
selfish, I think. But they've got a lot to give.

I don't know.

I guess it's strange to have so many people's hands inside
you as well. Rummaging around like wolves.

*Maybe towards the end of the monologue, 'Psycho Killer' by
Talking Heads has begun to play/fade up very quietly?*

*

ANNIE *stands alone on stage as the outro for 'Jesus Walks' plays.*

The crowd roars. The roars grow louder and louder until they are almost deafening. Maybe they transform from yells and whoops into a kind of beautiful choral hum? Maybe roses or feathers pour onto the stage.

ANNIE *breathes it in. She reaches her arms out to the side. Free.*

*

ANNIE *is speaking to the actress playing* EVE. *The audience should not know which character she is portraying.*

ANNIE. So apparently it doesn't happen all at once. The different parts of your body start shutting down at different times. It's basically every man for themselves, organ-wise. Like dominoes. So first your blood stops going round and starts to pool and *congeal*. So your body starts to go pink and purple. And then as your cells are like starved of oxygen, one by one, they begin to die. Slowly. Apparently the brain cells are the slowest. Neurons. It takes hours for them to go. And as the cells break down they attract fungi and bacteria and that bacteria starts eating up all your soft bits – organs and skin and stuff.

EVE. W/ow.

ANNIE. And – and so a lot of people think that your fingernails keep growing after you're dead. But actually they don't. Actually it's just the skin breaking? So the skin shrinks back and just exposes more of the nails that were underneath it. Yeah. And when your muscles relax – this is before rigor mortis hits – you just shit and piss everywhere. It all comes out of you. Apparently with guys their dick muscles can contract. So they get hard. Their dicks get hard. And sometimes, after death, they cum. Like they ejaculate. So they shit, piss and cum at the same time. That's what happens. That's what often happens.

Pause.

EVE. That's disgusting.

ANNIE. I'm sorry, baby. I'm being – that's weird isn't it?

EVE. Baby?

ANNIE. Kim – just forget I said that / – I was fucking around –
   I love you

EVE. *Kim?*… Annie, who are you speaking to?

   Beat. ANNIE *realises it's* EVE. *Maybe* EVE*'s clothes appear
   on her.*

ANNIE. Hi.

EVE. Why did you tell me all that?

ANNIE. I was reading about it.

EVE. I really wish you hadn't told me that.

ANNIE. It just will have been all over the bed or table or
   whatever she was on. All over the doctors' hands.

EVE. I don't get why it helps you to think about that.

ANNIE. Wasn't supposed to help.

   Pause.

   I'm not coming.

EVE. You're not coming?

ANNIE. I sorted the catering. There's gonna be like those mini
   burgers on brioche with like avocado in, and little salmon
   sashimi tostadas / and

EVE. What's a tostada?

ANNIE. It's Mexican.

EVE. Oh.

ANNIE. Mexican street food.

EVE. Right.

ANNIE. Crunchy kind of tortilla thing and then this little crazy-
   fresh piece of salmon on top. I think they put some crunchy
   onions on there too. Bit of Chipotle mayonnaise.

EVE. That sounds / really delicious.

ANNIE. There's gonna be hundreds of them.

EVE. Nice.

ANNIE. Yeah. I'll get thousands.

EVE. Thank you / for the tostadas.

ANNIE. You're welcome.

Pause.

EVE. But you're not coming?

ANNIE. No.

Pause.

EVE. Did that happen to you?

ANNIE. What?

EVE. When you died. Did you cum and piss and shit
everywhere?

ANNIE. Probably.

EVE. Kanye.

Silence.

If you're gonna do this – be this – I'm… out. We're done.
Like… yeah. We're done.

Beat.

ANNIE. Don't you want your money?

Pause.

EVE. I guess it's… you know it'd be horrible but… it's just sex.

It's not life or death.

Is it, baby?

ANNIE. What?

KIM. Is it, baby?

ANNIE. Evie?

> DIRECTOR *is played by the actor playing* ADAM. *The scene transforms around them. A studio.*

DIRECTOR. Um we're gonna start rolling. *Is* that okay, Kanye?

KIM. Kanye?

ANNIE. Yeah, baby.

> ANNIE *and* KIM *are stood behind a tub of face cream.*

DIRECTOR. The camera's just out there – (*Points to audience.*)

ANNIE (*squinting at audience*). Where?

DIRECTOR. And we're rolling

> KIM *takes a big lump of face cream and begins rubbing it into her face.* ANNIE *sees this and does the same.*

KIM. Oh my God.

ANNIE. Whoa.

KIM. That feels so good / on my skin.

ANNIE. Yeah. Um. Yeah. Yeah it feels like velvet. Feels like I'm rubbing a literal fucking cloud on my skin. (*To* DIRECTOR.) Oh you probably don't want us swearing?

DIRECTOR. Oh no no no we want this completely unfiltered. The Kim-Kanye experience.

ANNIE. Oh cool.

KIM. I can, like, feel my skin hydrating – like by the second?

ANNIE. Yeah I just wanna spread it all over my orifices.

> KIM *and* DIRECTOR *laugh. They apply more cream.*

> I wanna spread it all over *your* orifices.

KIM. We can do that!

> ANNIE *starts spreading the cream on* KIM.

DIRECTOR. This is great stuff. Do you mind if I – so sorry – the idea is that we just want to see you at your most natural and some of that will just be talking to each other and some of that will be talking to camera. Helen at the marketing firm just wants it to be as natural as possible.

ANNIE. Helen's a bitch.

Awkward pause. Then KIM *and* DIRECTOR *burst out laughing.* ANNIE *joins in.*

DIRECTOR. So yeah – let's just see what quotable stuff comes out.

KIM. Great.

DIRECTOR. I might throw in a couple of questions every now and then / to stimulate… whatever

ANNIE. Cool.   KIM. Totally cool. Kanye,
                                do you reckon if people
                                use this face cream they'll
                                be like – immortal like
                                you are?

I mean it's good face cream, baby, but it's… But maybe if you use enough of it?

ANNIE *dumps a HUGE dollop of face cream on* KIM's *face. Laughs.*

DIRECTOR. How do you get resurrected, Kanye?

ANNIE. I think you just gotta believe in yourself enough. Like if you *believe* that you're better than death than maybe you will be?

DIRECTOR. Great.

ANNIE. I'm not interested in death. All death is very boring to me.

KIM (*wiping cream away*). We're very lucky. Like, if Kanye hadn't been the second Messiah I'd be raising our two beautiful children on my own. And that would've had very real effects on their like – development?

ANNIE. I reckon if we had another kid now, they'd have like magic powers or some shit. He'd be like crawling up walls or turnin' fucking yogurt into wine, or feeding a load of people outside our house.

KIM. I think we're good with the ones we got though. For now.

ANNIE. Yeah.

KIM. They can be a handful right? But we love them.

ANNIE. Yeah. Plus I like, just got Kim's vagina looking how I want it to look so let's not push another life-form through it too soon.

KIM. Don't do that.

ANNIE. I'm just kidding, baby.

KIM. I know but I don't find that funny. Can we edit that bit out please / otherwise my people are going to have words to say.

DIRECTOR. Yeah, sure.

ANNIE. Sorry, baby.

KIM. It's okay.

ANNIE. No I'm sorry – I hate it when men talk about women that way.

KIM. He's so feminist.

ANNIE (*to herself*). I am a feminist.

KIM. And it's just as good on black skin as it is on white skin isn't it Kanye?

ANNIE. Um yeah. Sure. Yeah it's a… it's a colourblind face cream. It doesn't see race.

DIRECTOR. That's great. I love that.

KIM *slaps a huge dollop of face cream on* ANNIE*'s face. Laughs. Wipes it off.*

Sorry I've just got the execs in my ear. They um – sorry –

Pause. DIRECTOR *motions to his ear and indicates that the
agency execs are going on a bit.*

ANNIE *turns to* KIM *and they smile at each other, warmly.*
KIM *leans in and pushes a strand of* ANNIE*'s hair back.*
ANNIE*'s eyes widen.*

Okay so the big bosses at the agency are apparently really
hoping to appeal to the black market.

Beeping in DIRECTOR*'s ear. He winces.*

Yep okay – Sorry not the illegal market – the market of black
people – black face-cream buyers.

KIM. Okay.

DIRECTOR. So they just wanna see you try that.

ANNIE. Um. I dunno how that would work. Like um / black
people want the same things as everyone else.

DIRECTOR. Okay um so let's… so: Kanye do you think um…
do you think the response to your resurrection would have
been different if you weren't a black guy? D'ya wanna just
rub the…

ANNIE *rubs in the cream.*

Do you think people find the idea of an African American
Messiah hard to process or…?

ANNIE. I um – you know – I can't answer that. I'm just doing
me. I'm just being me – I'm not a… And this face cream is
a fucking great way to be yourself. You know I glow when
I wear it?

DIRECTOR. That's great –   KIM. Yeah, you do. You look
    that's awesome – but like   all… sexy and…
    just between you and me I
    think they want you to just
    black it up a bit?

ANNIE. 'Black it up a bit'?

DIRECTOR. Yeah. That's basically what they're saying. /
Trying to be PC about it but

ANNIE. Why do I have to black it up, man? Why do I have to
be 'an African American Messiah'? I'm just me. I'm just
doing me – I'm a *me Messiah*.

DIRECTOR. This is great stuff.

ANNIE. I just wanna tell people that, you know, I am not
defined by the colour of my fucking skin. You know what,
fuck *you*, for for defining me that way. Don't put a box on
me, man. I am not *just* a black man.

KIM. Kanye.

ANNIE. No I am not *just* a black man, bro. I am not *just* a –

A rush of voices. Maybe ANNIE *keeps trying to talk over
them but we can't hear it.*

*

ANNIE *stands centre-stage.*

ANNIE. There's a crack.

Just here.

We need a new wall.

KIM. Where?

ANNIE. Just here.

Look.

Feel it.

Stuff's coming in.

I can hear it.

There's a muttering.

Sipping… sipping of drinks

Chewing and inhaling.

KIM. Kanye. You okay, babe?

ANNIE. Yeah. I need to get some – it's called Polyfilla isn't it? The stuff you use to fill in cracks? Holes.

KIM. Babe.

ANNIE. Maybe I could just use some tissues. Or some pillows. Or maybe just the feathers inside the pillows.

KIM. Kanye. Norie wants to tell you a story.

ANNIE. What story?

KIM. Something about you probably. Like normal. Last night she went on and on about you fighting a dragon with your bare hands. Killing an evil king.

KIM *kisses (or tries to kiss)* ANNIE *but* ANNIE *pulls away.*

Whoa.

Pause. ANNIE *goes over to a piano. She awkwardly plays/tries to remember one of those songs EVERYONE knew on the piano as a kid – 'Chopsticks', 'Heart and Soul' or similar. She fumbles it.*

KIM *laughs.*

ANNIE *shushes her, harshly. She tries the tune again.*

What are you doing?

ANNIE *stops.*

Babe.

ANNIE. Yo I'mma go hear a story
    From Norie
    Get me some glory
    Better not be boring
    That's a half-rhyme
    Ah well. That's fine.
    Damn, look at the time
    It's not even half-past nine

KIM. It's eight.

ANNIE. Yeah.

Pause.

They're saying stuff about me

KIM. Who are?

ANNIE. The people on the... behind the – talking about...

KIM. People always talk.

ANNIE. Saying I'm embarrassed to be black.

Saying I'm self-obsessed.

Saying I abandoned them.

Saying they want me dead.

KIM. He shouldn't have released that.

ANNIE. Saying I killed / her.

KIM. Kanye.

Look at me.

Pause.

ANNIE. I remember all the boys watching your sex tape in school. They had it on their phones.

KIM. What?

ANNIE. Sorry that was – That was – I was just thinking about a lyric.

KIM. ...okay?

ANNIE. You look amazing.

KIM. I wasn't looking for that.

ANNIE. You're a goddess, baby. You're like everything I...

KIM. Stop.

Just talk to me, okay?

Beat.

ANNIE. I'll get some stuff to fix this tomorrow – the crack –
    but right now I'm – I'm just gonna go listen to Norie's story.

Pause.

KIM. I need you to start treating me like I'm real.

*

*A rush of voices. Mindless chatter. They build to a deafening
cacophony. ANNIE winces at the volume.*

She turns to find MANAGER eating a lot of grapes.

ANNIE. I need to do something.

MANAGER. Okay.

ANNIE. Make something to…

MANAGER. You mean like an album?

ANNIE. Yeah like an album. People love albums don't they?

MANAGER. Sure.

ANNIE. When you signed me did you like… Were people
    excited?

MANAGER. Yeah?

ANNIE. Did they – your family – did they

MANAGER. What?

ANNIE. I dunno.

MANAGER. Okay well…

ANNIE. What did your mum think – was she happy?

Beat.

MANAGER. I told you to never mention that bitch again.

ANNIE. Oh. Sorry. I didn't know.

MANAGER. FUCK.

ANNIE. Whoa.

Silence. ANNIE *stares at him, shocked.*

Eventually:

MANAGER. Have you got any ideas?

Beat.

ANNIE. That's how I usually start?

MANAGER. Yeah.

ANNIE. With an idea.

MANAGER.... Yeah.

ANNIE. Okay. Well yeah – yeah I've got something.

MANAGER. Great. Like a sound that you're interested in?

ANNIE. No I can't... do that

MANAGER. Or a hook – a super-catchy hook.

ANNIE. I've got a visual. I wanna start with a visual this time.

MANAGER. Okay.

ANNIE. Uh. So. So it's based on this time I climbed up
    Kilimanjaro.

MANAGER. Great.

ANNIE. So there's this mountain.

MANAGER. Mountain.

ANNIE. Yeah. And I'm at the top of it. And there are all these
    women running round it. Tribal women. I want them all
    running round it and climbing up it. And the ones climbing
    up it are beautiful and smart. They're dressed like ballerinas
    but they've got PhDs too. And wings! Not dainty little shitty
    fucking angel wings, proper eagle, *albatross* wings made of
    feathers. Real feathers. And then the ones at the bottom are
    monsters. Like goblins. Goblins yeah. They've got these
    claws and shit. They've got boils on their faces and pus
    coming out of them. And they've got massive glowing dicks.
    Yeah. They've got massive erect fucking penises that glow.

Even the women. They're at the bottom. And they're waiting for the angels to fall so they can fucking eat them. Or rape them. Yeah. Rape is scarier. So they can rape the angels. And I'm at the top on my own. It's just me. I'm the first one up. At the top of the mountain. Just this figure looking down on everything. Alone. I'm just checking it out. I'm not climbing – I'm just checking it out.

Pause.

MANAGER. Okay.

ANNIE. It's good right?

MANAGER. Yeah.

ANNIE. No no no. Don't look at me like that. Adam, look at me like I'm

MANAGER. Who's Adam?

ANNIE. Nobody.

Pause.

MANAGER. I don't see a lot of money here.

Maybe the video of the hamster doing backflips appears.
ANNIE *watches it.*

MANAGER *can't see it.*

MANAGER *starts to walk away.*

ANNIE. I wanna...

I wanna start making hats.

MANAGER. Hats?

ANNIE. Fashion hats.

I wanna start making and wearing fashion hats.

That's the new direction.

That's who I am.

*

*ANNIE is doubled over a table with her back to the audience.
She is working on a hat that we cannot see.*

Smoke and light pour out of the hat.

Lightning and fire pour out of the hat.

*Maybe it starts to snow? In slow motion? The snow slowly turns
into thousands of white feathers.*

*ANNIE raises the hat above her head. It looks a lot like
a crown and is the strangest and most wondrous hat you've
ever seen.*

A choir of angels sing a high note.

*She brings it down onto her head. The second she does so,
Smokey Robinson's 'The Tracks of My Tears' begins to play.*

*When the vocal line kicks in, ANNIE spins round and begins
dancing/mouthing to it.*

*The actors that play EVE and ADAM are on stage. They are
dancing together. They mouth/dance through the song with huge
smiles on their faces. The actress of MOTHER runs in from the
audience, embraces ANNIE and joins in.*

*Maybe they all hug each other passionately towards the end,
kissing each other on the cheek, not letting go, clinging on?*

*

Actress playing EVE does ANNIE's make-up.

*ANNIE stares into her eyes as she does so. ANNIE is wearing
the crown hat and probably a long, regal-looking cloak as well.*

MAKE-UP ASSISTANT. Okay.

ANNIE. Yeah I'm ready. My face looks…?

   MAKE-UP ASSISTANT *nods.*

MAKE-UP ASSISTANT. You look great

ANNIE. Yeah?

MAKE-UP ASSISTANT. Yeah.

A warm pause.

ANNIE. Thank you.

MAKE-UP ASSISTANT. No it's a… it's an honour, sir.

   Beat. ANNIE's *smile fades.*

   Is everything okay?

ANNIE. Yeah, I just – I thought I recognised you for a second.

MAKE-UP ASSISTANT. Sorry.

ANNIE. What's his name?

MAKE-UP ASSISTANT. Who – the…?

ANNIE. Mmm.

MAKE-UP ASSISTANT. Michael Parkinson.

ANNIE. Michael Parkinson.

MAKE-UP ASSISTANT. Good luck.

   ANNIE *smiles at* MAKE-UP ASSISTANT.

   PARKINSON *is played by the actress that plays* MOTHER.
   ANNIE's *face goes pale, as if she has just seen a ghost.*

PARKINSON. Hi, Kanye. I'm Michael.

ANNIE. Mum.

PARKINSON. It's so lovely to meet you. I'm really excited that
   we've got this chance to have a chat. So good that we could
   make it work.

   Pause.

   You okay, Kanye?

ANNIE. Yeah.

PARKINSON. What is it?

ANNIE. You're a ghost.

   PARKINSON *laughs heartily.*

PARKINSON. Oh God do I look it?

My doctor keeps telling me I need more Vitamin D.

That's the one that's in sunlight isn't it?

Kanye?

Silence.

ANNIE. Sorry.

PARKINSON. Not at all. You alright?

ANNIE. Yeah I just – you look like someone I haven't seen in a while.

PARKINSON (*laughing*). Alright alright! I know I haven't been around for a bit.

PARKINSON *laughs heartily.*

Okay shall we get down to it.

ANNIE. Sure.

Suddenly huge lights come on and the interview has begun.

PARKINSON. Can I tell you something Kanye?

Can I confess something to you?

ANNIE. Yeah, Mum – MAN.

PARKINSON. I have never before interviewed somebody who has been resurrected.

ANNIE. Yeah we're pretty few and far between.

PARKINSON. That's very exciting for me.

ANNIE. Yeah I get that.

You know it's pretty exciting for me too.

I never knew anyone else that got resurrected.

And I get to be around me all the time!

PARKINSON. So that stays exciting?

ANNIE. Yeah that don't get boring.

PARKINSON. I like the hat you're wearing today by the way

ANNIE. Thank you.

PARKINSON. It's lovely.

ANNIE. Yeah you think so?

I did this.

I designed this hat. And I did it all by myself.

PARKINSON. Wow. That's impressive.

FAN (*from audience*). Oh fuck that, man!

FAN *is standing somewhere in the audience*. PARKINSON *and* ANNIE *are blinded by the lights and can't see him initially.*

PARKINSON. Who said that?

FAN. Kanye! Why / you doing that, man?

PARKINSON. Who is that? Security can you...?

ANNIE. Who are you?

A tussle.

FAN. Kanye! You remember   PARKINSON. Sorry about
me right?   this Kanye. This very
                                                          rarely happens.

ANNIE (*to audience*). Dad?

FAN. Kanye, I just wanna talk.

ANNIE (*to* PARKINSON). Leave him. Can you just – / let him – Dad?

FAN. I just wanna have a conversation. I just wanna ask if you're okay.

PARKINSON. Is this okay, Kanye?

ANNIE. This has happened before.

PARKINSON. What, Kanye?

ANNIE. There's –

this is

They're falling down outside.

We were supposed to be at football.

PARKINSON. Football, Kanye?

ANNIE. I haven't seen you together.

Since he left. Never seen you

together

PARKINSON. Kanye. You alright?

Pause. ANNIE *tries to pull herself together.*

ANNIE. Do you have any water?

PARKINSON. Can we get Kanye some water?

Actress of EVE *brings on some water.*

She squeezes ANNIE'*s shoulder as she leaves.*

FAN. It's Taylor. You remember me. I didn't believe you were real until you came up to me at the bar.

ANNIE *looks after her.*

FAN. We went back to yours.

ANNIE. Taylor. Sorting me out.

FAN. So you're in the hat business now?

Beat.

ANNIE. Yes.

FAN. Rapper, Messiah, hat-maker.

ANNIE. Yes.

FAN. Why are you doing that, man? I don't know why you're doing that.

Pause.

ANNIE. People look really good in hats.

People feel so good when they're wearing a good hat.

PARKINSON. Very true.

FAN. How much you selling them for?

ANNIE. I'm um… like really good prices.

FAN. I guess poor kids aren't gonna be wearing them to school.

Beat.

ANNIE. You don't… you don't you don't own me, okay? You think cos you know the words to my songs, you you you control me? You don't even know me. / You *left* me.

FAN. I do know you.

ANNIE. You know *a version* of me.

FAN. I liked that version.

ANNIE. That version changed. It changes. I'm not something that is that is that is… *finished*. Even if you want me to be. I was a rapper. Then I was the Messiah. Now I'm a hat-maker.

FAN. What's wrong with hip hop?

ANNIE. Hat-making's the new hip hop.

PARKINSON. 'Hat-making's the new hip hop' – I like that.

FAN. Why weren't you at the marches, man?

You know how many of your songs we played there?

We basically did the whole discography. Top to bottom.	ANNIE. Whoa – okay –
What better thing did you have to do that day?	Look I can't take every bullet.
Donda would've been there. Your mum would've been there.	

ANNIE *stares at* PARKINSON.

ANNIE. That's not my responsibility.

FAN. Then what *is* your responsibility, man? You don't get to just take the good bits.

ANNIE. I'm not taking the good bits.

FAN. It's a loss, man. This thing? It's a loss.

ANNIE. Oh 'it's a loss'. 'It's a loss.' Mum – Michael Parkinson. 'it's a loss'.

What have you *lost*? You don't know what loss is.

You know what I don't get – why did nobody go up to Steve Jobs, Picasso, Warhol and go 'it's a loss you got new shit now'. Nobody went: man the iMac is good but don't you dare start making phones. Don't you dare start making the most beloved family movies of all time. OF ALL TIME.

PARKINSON. So are / you saying

ANNIE. *NEMO*.

   NEMO.

PARKINSON. It's a great movie.

ANNIE. It's a great fucking movie.

PARKINSON. So are you / saying

FAN. He's saying we're being racist.

ANNIE. NO. No, all I'm / saying

PARKINSON. You're saying white musicians, celebrities.

FAN. Gods.

ANNIE. I'm saying: I AM WARHOL. Let me be Warhol. If you just let me me leave this fucking house I can be Warhol

PARKINSON. You're saying white artists aren't expected to have a representational responsibility in the same way that black artists are.

ANNIE. No, what I am saying is that – is that, to you, I'm not the main character. I'm just a tiny cameo part in your whole fucking existence. I'm the guy digging the graves at the end. I'm the guy on the screen in the background. I'm the kid in the booth while the towers go down. I'm not *real* to you. But those people change too bro. They change too. And you people – you call yourselves communities, you call yourself 'families' but you're just – you're just holding us back.

PARKINSON. You're saying that black artists are required to think about their communities and their families in ways that white artists aren't.

ANNIE. No I didn't say that. Listen

FAN. You're so full of excuses, man.

PARKINSON (*to* FAN). Let him speak / or I will have you removed.

It's always *you* this or *you* that

Someone's always fucking *you* over

ANNIE. Look look look I'mma let you finish but

PARKINSON. Do you think you're an example of that, Kanye?

ANNIE. Of what?

PARKINSON. Of thinking about your community. Your family.

Pause.

ANNIE. You know what *you* never understood, Mum.

You know what neither of you – none of you – ever understood

PARKINSON. Mum?

They don't need racism any more.

Okay.

They don't need sexism   Sexism?
any more.

They don't need wealth or
or prejudice.

They don't need any of that
to hold us back.   FAN. Who?

Any more.   Who you talking about?

They got this new thing

It's called: Self-Hate.

It works on itself – it's automatic.

They been working on it since the seventies and it's like the best investment they've got.

It's like the real estate of prejudice. It kills protest – revolution – all of it – dead.

And it's just like if I say if I say: I Am A God.

The voice in the back of my head goes: Who does she think she is?

And you guys, Mum, you guys make that voice sing louder and louder and louder.

You're smart about it: 'yeah you can do it. Yeah you can do it.'

Like you're training your puppy. Happy clappy. But inside it's just:

Who does she think she is

Cos I don't trust it any more.

Who does she think she is

Who does she think she is

She sings that phrase.

I just told you who I thought I was: A god.

I just told you. That's who I think I am.

Would it be better if I had a song that said: I am a nigga.

Or if I had a song that said I am a gangsta.

Or I am a pimp. I am a bitch. Slut.

All those names fit better on a person like me right?

When I wrote a song called 'Monster'. When I say:
'Everybody knows I'm a motherfuckin' monster' you all
sit there sipping your fucking Starbucks saying 'yeah she is
a monster.'

But to say you're a god.

FAN. You know other people exist, man? / We're real too. Look
outside of your own problems for a second.

PARKINSON. You're saying that people put you in boxes /
because you're a black man.

ANNIE. To say you're a hat-maker. Cos I am a hat-maker.
I make hats.

FAN. You're being a fucking coward.

ANNIE. YOU DON'T GET IT, YOU DON'T HAVE THE
ANSWERS

PARKINSON. And what do you think gives you the right to
talk about this? Because it feels slightly like you're trying
to make excuses.

ANNIE. I'm not making excuses. Everyone – everyone –
everyone thinks I'm just in it for me.

Everyone thinks I am just in it for Kanye West.

But they don't get that by *being* me, by doing what I'm
doing, by saying what I'm saying, I *am* defeating it. I *am*
defeating racism, classism, sexism, homophobia. I *am* doing
that by being me.

Because they don't want anybody to be themselves and to be
happy about that.

Their whole system relies on it. That's what makes it go
round.

Know what, if you're a Kanye West fan, you're not a fan of me, you're a fan of yourself.

I am doing this *for* you. I became me *for* you.

I am doing this so that when you piss yourself in public you don't have to hurt no more.

PARKINSON. Really?

ANNIE. Yes.

PARKINSON. And do you think that is an act of love, Kanye?

Silence. There are tears in ANNIE*'s eyes by this point.*

FAN. We *miss* you, man

PARKINSON. Kanye. Do you think that is an act of love?

ANNIE. Yes.

FAN. We want you back, Kanye.

ANNIE. Yes I think it's an act of love.

And that's why – that's why – that's why I wanna run for Prime Minister of this country.

FAN. Oh for fuck's sake.

PARKINSON. Wow! Of Great Britain?

ANNIE. Yeah of Great Britain. I think Great Britain could be even greater than it already is.

PARKINSON. So which party will you join?

ANNIE. I'm a – I'm a independent.

PARKINSON. Well, to be Prime Minister you need to be leader of the party that gets the most number of seats in Parliament so you can't be Prime Minister if you're an independent.

ANNIE. Well I'm gonna join one of the parties.

PARKINSON. And what constituency will you run in?

ANNIE. Um.

PARKINSON. What seat will you contest?

FAN. Yeah, Kanye West for Bromley and Chislehurst.

ANNIE. I'm not sure yet. I'm not sure. It's just an idea.

I'm just *trying*.

I'm just fucking *trying*.

Please.

FAN. You're not / trying

PARKINSON. Let him speak.

FAN. Don't you feel guilty?

ANNIE. I FEEL GUILTY ALL THE TIME

Pause.

don't you think – don't you think that – that – that I *know* it's my fault?

don't you think i *know* that?

of course i *know* it's all my fault.

you leaving and you dying

all of you being being let down, betrayed – not clapping

like i *know* that.

cos i'm not stupid

at least

i'm not – i'm not like…

i'm not stupid

i'm not fucking stupid am i?

i'm not.

Silence.

sorry

PARKINSON. No –

ANNIE. no – listen –

I miss you and I'm sorry.

Beat.

PARKINSON. No Kanye, this is really great television. We can edit it down if you want us to but I think this could be really good for the both of us. Recently advertisers have – you know – started questioning their investment seeing as I haven't 'technically' been on television for over a decade now so this could be

PARKINSON*'s voice fades to silence.*

*

ANNIE. Mum?

Where are you?

Please, if you're – I need to talk to you.

A blinding light shines down from above. Terrifying music plays.

VOICE OF KANYE. Hello White Kanye.

The VOICE OF KANYE *is made up of samples of the man himself's voice. It should be obvious that the samples have been cobbled together from different sources.*

ANNIE. Who are you?

VOICE OF KANYE. I'm Kanye West. Who the fuck are you?

ANNIE. I'm you.

VOICE OF KANYE. You ain't nothing like me. You're a fucking fake. You disgust me, White Kanye.

ANNIE. Then why did you choose me, man?

VOICE OF KANYE. And there I was thinking y'all stopped painting your faces in the sixties.

ANNIE. You did this to me! This is all your fault!

VOICE OF KANYE. My fault? One moment I'm down there minding my own business and then I'm up here and there's this phony white chick on Earth using my body, playing my songs, taking care of my family, taking my story and saying it's hers. My fault? You pushed me out.

ANNIE. Whoa I didn't push you out. I didn't choose any of this. If it wasn't you it was someone else.

VOICE OF KANYE. At some point along the way you seem to have made some choices, white girl.

ANNIE. Well I can't remember how that happened / – I just woke up.

VOICE OF KANYE. Sometimes we like to forget the means we take to gain power.

ANNIE. Stop / saying that.

VOICE OF KANYE. I came here to tell you something, Kanye The Second.

It's part of this – we're doing this Unburdening Week thing up here.

Lots of breathing and trust exercises and airing our feelings and so...

ANNIE. What?

VOICE OF KANYE. Well I came here to tell you that they will always know. Kim and the kids.

They'll pretend they don't. Every time they look at you they'll smile.

But deep down they'll know.

And I feel sorry for you for that, White Kanye.

ANNIE. That's not true.

VOICE OF KANYE *begins laughing maniacally.*

KIM. Kanye.

ANNIE. That's not true.

KIM. What happened to you on there? I tried to get on stage but
    they wouldn't let me.

ANNIE. You're lying. You don't know.

KIM. It's crazy they let that idiot shout at you for so long.

ANNIE. Can I ask you something?

VOICE OF KANYE. God no.

ANNIE. Oh okay.

KIM. Unacceptable actually. I'll get people on it. But you
    looked so sad baby.

VOICE OF KANYE. Oh fuck it go on then.

ANNIE. What's heaven like?

KIM. Babe, you alright?

VOICE OF KANYE. I'm not really sure.

    It's kind of like a warm bath.

    The voice glitches and fizzles out.

ANNIE. Are you still there?

KIM. Yeah, I'm right here.

    ANNIE *turns to* KIM.

ANNIE. Kim let's get out of here. Let's just drive and and and
    let's go hiking! I think we should go hiking! Do you have
    hiking boots?

KIM. Kanye, slow down.

ANNIE. I'm gonna buy you some hiking boots. I'm gonna buy
    the kids some hiking boots and we are gonna get out of this
    place and go *hiking* – YAY!

KIM. Baby, you're not making any sense. What happened on
    that show?

ANNIE. Nothing happened. I just wanna be somewhere else now. It'll just be us – our family. You can / understand that – you get that.

KIM. We can go wherever but just talk to me for a second.

ANNIE. I don't want to talk to you – that's not why you're here. Start packing.

KIM puts her head in her hands and crouches down, breathing deeply. ANNIE watches, confused.

KIM. I can't do this.

ANNIE. What? Hiking? I will carry your bags, babe.

Pause.

You don't believe me.

KIM. Believe you?

ANNIE. That I'm me.

KIM. It's got nothing to do with that, Kanye.

Silence.

ANNIE. I wanna see your tape.

KIM. What?

ANNIE. I wanna see what you look like when you're…

Where is it? You digitised them. I remember.

KIM. What?

ANNIE. You digitised them.

No.

The photo albums.

KIM. What the fuck are you talking about?

ANNIE. The tape. The tape of you.

ANNIE begins watching KIM's sex tape.

KIM. Don't watch that.

Why would you watch that?

That is so weird.

That is so fucking insulting.

ANNIE. Everyone else has seen it.

KIM. They don't know me. They're not married to me.

ANNIE. They think they know you.

KIM. Who gives a fuck what they think. What is wrong with you?

ANNIE. This is disgusting.

KIM. It's just sex.

ANNIE. How can *you* be doing *that*?

KIM. Because I wanted to.

ANNIE. You're a goddess.

KIM. No I'm not.

ANNIE. You're the most / beautiful

KIM. Why don't we have sex any more?

ANNIE. No – stop.

KIM. Why don't we have sex any more, Kanye?

ANNIE. Has Mum seen it? I bet Mum's seen it.

KIM. Mum?

ANNIE. I bet she has, Evie. I bet she judges you for it.

KIM. Who's Evie.

ANNIE. Evie.

KIM. Who's Evie, Kanye?

ANNIE. My sister.

Evie's my sister

KIM. You don't have a sister. Who is she?

Some fan.

Some whore you've been fucking.

ANNIE. No I do.

She had a tape.

Just like you.

It was – you

It's you.

Evie.

KIM. Who the fuck's Evie, Kanye?

ANNIE. You're right here.

KIM. You're losing your mind.

ANNIE. She's you. She's…

You look so much like her.

She was perfect too.

She was…

So beautiful.   JONATHAN *enters,*
                                        played by the actor playing
Evie?   ADAM.

                                        KIM. Jonathan, / Kanye's
                                        having a breakdown.

JONATHAN. Kim, is everything okay? What's going on?

ANNIE. What are you doing here?

KIM. Jonathan. Kanye's going crazy.

ANNIE. No you're my…

I fucked you and my dick glowed

JONATHAN. What?

ANNIE. You had a cancellation. You eat all my grapes.

KIM. You're dangerous.   JONATHAN. Kim, what the

　　I want you to leave.   fuck's going on?

ANNIE. You're everyone. / Both of you. Reminding me –
　　always

KIM. Kanye I want you to leave. Jonathan, go get help. Call an
　　ambulance, police.

JONATHAN. *Police?*

KIM. Just / do it.

　　JONATHAN *runs off.* ANNIE *has been grasping at the hat*
　　on her head. As she touches it, it either turns to dust? or
　　becomes a messy collection of twigs?

　　Kanye. Look at me.

ANNIE. Kim. / I feel sick – dizzy.

KIM. I want you to leave this house. Now.

　　Just for a bit.

ANNIE. It's like everyone's watching us.

KIM. Kanye.

ANNIE. Your tape. In your tape.

KIM. Listen to me.

ANNIE. It's like there are all these faces watching us.
　　Even when we think we're alone.

KIM. LISTEN TO ME

ANNIE. Except it's not me they're watching.

　　It's him.

KIM. Who?

　　Kanye, who?

ANNIE. They don't get to watch.

KIM. Kanye

ANNIE. That's not my name.

KIM. I need you to get out now.

ANNIE. You don't get to watch.

> *Maybe* ANNIE *goes to unplug the lights to the theatre?*
> *Some of them power down.* KIM *picks up the same weapon*
> EVE *wielded against* ANNIE *after her initial*
> *transformation.*

KIM. GET THE FUCK OUT OF MY HOUSE I DON'T
RECOGNISE YOU ANY MORE.

> ANNIE *stares at her, wide-eyed.*

*

ANNIE stands centre-stage on her own with a heavily vocoded
microphone and a synth pad. She is dressed in a costume that
obscures her entire body and face.

The crowd roars. The beat for 'Wolves' by Kanye West plays.

ANNIE. Hello?

> *Crowd shouts: 'Hello!'*

> (*As if calling for a specific voice.*) Can you hear me?

> *Crowd shouts: 'YES!'*

> (*Again.*) Not you I don't want you.

> *Crowd laughs and cheers.*

> I woulda given you that money, bro.
> I promise I would've.
> I bought that fucking Mexican shit. Thousands of them.
> Evie, just call me, bro.
> I know you're after me.

> *The beat for 'Wolves' dies out.*

I know you got people gunning for me. I can hear them.
Please don't send them at my head.
Just call me, bro.
Let's just talk. Let's just talk to each other.

Boos. Someone heckles: 'Sing us a song.'

*The intro to 'Pinocchio Story' by Kanye West starts to play.
She sings the first verse and chorus of the song through a
vocoded microphone.*

ANNIE *then descends into a half-singing half-speaking
freestyle that ends with her chanting: 'I FEEL SO MUCH
LOVE TONIGHT' into the cheering crowd. This is taken
from Kanye West's performance at The Hollywood Bowl
in 2015.*

ANNIE*'s words slur and become general unintelligible
mumblings over the music. This can continue as the next
scene is being set.*

*

*A kids' club booth. At the top of a mountain. There is a swan-
shaped ball pit. Maybe some cones are scattered around. Or
some bibs. Maybe an Arsenal Bergkamp shirt is thrown on the
floor somewhere. The whole place should feel warm. A banner
reads: 'KIDS' CLUB'.*

DAD *is played by the actor that plays* ADAM. LUCY *is played
by the actress that plays* EVE. LUCY *speaks in an Irish accent.*
LUCY *spends the first half of the scene clearing up the clutter.*

*Maybe a screen flickers with old footage of Parkinson
interviews with famous, smiling stars of yesteryear. David
Bowie, Muhammad Ali, Meg Ryan.*

ANNIE *enters. Maybe she is wearing a snow-covered coat and
hiking boots.*

ANNIE. Hi.

DAD *nods. He is sipping a pint or a whiskey.*

LUCY. Hiya there. Have a sit down, love.

Pause. ANNIE *does.* LUCY *sings country songs under her breath as she clears.*

ANNIE. I've been climbing for hours. Wasn't expecting anyone else to be up here.

DAD. It's worth it for the views. You can see down the whole mountain.

ANNIE. I don't really know why I came. I just started climbing.

DAD *and* LUCY *exchange a glance. Maybe they giggle a bit.*

ANNIE. What?

DAD. No don't worry. It's just Lucy here said the exact same thing when she first dropped by.

LUCY. Pretty much word for word now wasn't it!

DAD. Word for fucking word!

They giggle.

LUCY. Sorry, love.

ANNIE. No.

I've been here before. But it wasn't on top of a mountain. It was in a football club.

LUCY. Mmmm.

DAD. Quiet isn't it?

Pause. ANNIE *listens.*

ANNIE. Yeah.

DAD. Away from all the chaos.

A sudden swell of noise from outside the booth.

Screams/sirens/buzz. They all look up at the ceiling nervously. It dies down.

ANNIE. You look just like my dad.

DAD. Oh yeah?

ANNIE. Yeah.

DAD. Lucky man.

ANNIE. He's an insurance salesman.

DAD. I'm an insurance salesman.

ANNIE. I thought you were.

LUCY. Tony doesn't like to talk about work while he's here.
It makes him very upset.

DAD. 'Upset.'

> DAD *and* LUCY *share a smile*.

ANNIE. Why does it make you upset?

DAD. Lucy's mothering me.

> I guess I just always wanted to be a bit of a hero.

> You know a cowboy or a surgeon – something silly like that.

> And I realised, eventually, that that was never going to
> happen.

> I'm rotten inside you see. Nothing to be done.

> Sorry, I know we've only just met.

LUCY. Tony doesn't really like to talk about it.

ANNIE. My dad's name is Tony.

DAD. Lucy was just telling me about her existential crisis.

ANNIE. Oh sorry for interrupting.

LUCY. No bother, love.

ANNIE. Love?

DAD. Lucy's been fooling around with two young lads.

LUCY. Shush!

DAD. Best friends no less. Torn them apart no less.

ANNIE. Really?

LUCY. I've fucked everything up if I'm honest with you. Two lovely boys. Chris and Adam. Chris and I were seeing each other. Had been for a while. I'd met his parents – they took me out sailing actually. Which was nice cos I'd never been before.

DAD (*to* ANNIE). You ever been sailing?

ANNIE. Once with my dad when I was very little. We went up to the Lake District for a May bank holiday and he rented a boat and he tried to teach me how to sail a little bit. He couldn't sail. He just liked the idea of it I think.

Pause. DAD *stares at* ANNIE. *She gazes back.*

DAD. Ann/ie?

ANNIE (*to* LUCY). Carry on – I want to hear the rest of your story.

LUCY. Tony are / you

DAD *keeps gazing at* ANNIE *for a moment then shakes himself out of it.*

DAD. Yes. Go on dear.

LUCY. So me and Chris were happy together for a while. I felt so comfortable and so safe with him. Like I was totally myself I think. But he has this best friend called Adam. Adam's not really my type looks-wise. He has these blue eyes and this long, curly blonde hair which I've always found a bit silly. But then one night he uh we'd been drinking and Chris was in one corner of the room playing an Oasis song on the guitar and Adam just came up to me and whispered 'I've wanted to tell you this for ages but I think you are the most beautiful person ever. I think you're like: *TV* beautiful.' I'm really not wanting to show off here.

DAD. No.

LUCY. I'm just trying to tell the story as accurately as possible.

DAD. Keep going.

LUCY. And that just kind of rang around my head for a bit. Those words. And I turned around and looked up at him. We started sleeping together a few nights later. And it felt like something completely outside of my realm of understanding. But at the same time so... *real*? It was like I was finally the... you know cos I'm just nobody really. But then obviously it all got out and Chris tried to kill Adam. Not literally. But they did punch each other a few times. Knocked each other out. I arrived and they were both passed out on the floor of Adam's flat. And um...

ANNIE (*croaky voice*). What?

LUCY. Well, I guess I was looking at them on the floor – these two lovely boys with big purple bruises on their heads – and I realised that for them, it was never really about me. And I guess, for me it was never really about them. And I couldn't really stand there for very long. My stomach was all queasy with it, you see.

Cos I look at everyone – you know I always know what everyone's up to. And there just seems like there is so much joy and so much adoration in the world. And then also so much hate and so much loathing. People are just expressin' themselves so purely. And I love it. I – you know – I *applaud* it – it's so important. But when *I'm* angry it doesn't feel like that. And when I'm in love – when I felt like I loved someone – when they were camped out in my head all the time – it... it didn't feel like it looks like it should feel. There's always this thing in me. This weight – *noise* that won't stop.

Sorry that's pretty muddled.

I think more than anything else, I just want *my* love to look like *their* love. I think that's it. And if it did, if it really did, I'd be completely fine. I think then I'd be totally okay.

DAD *squeezes* LUCY*'s hand. Maybe* LUCY *rests her head on* DAD*'s shoulder.*

Long silence.

ANNIE. Sorry.

Can I ask you guys something?

DAD. Sure.   LUCY. Mmmm.

ANNIE. What do you see when you look at me?

Pause.

DAD. I see a very frightened young woman.

Beat.

ANNIE. That's what I used to see.

LUCY. And now?

ANNIE. Now I just see Kanye West.

Pause.

DAD. He's married to that woman. The one with the – with the ginormous bottom. I watched her video. The things she does with her mouth.

Pause. ANNIE*'s heart breaks. She stares at* DAD.

ANNIE. You should be better than this, Dad.

DAD. I know.

*

ANNIE *shuts all the lights in the theatre off.*

She lights a torch and turns it towards centre-stage where there is a child's bed. Kanye's daughter North (four years old) lies in the bed. North's dialogue plays over the speaker. Maybe it distorts, pans and glitches around?

ANNIE. North, baby. You gotta come with me okay? Daddy's getting you out of here.

VOICE OF NORTH. Where are we going?

ANNIE. I'm getting you somewhere safe, baby. Somewhere we can be together. Away from all of this.

VOICE OF NORTH. I'm sleepy, Daddy.

ANNIE. That's okay. You can sleep in the car.

VOICE OF NORTH. Okay, Daddy.

ANNIE. Yep that's it. Come on. Up we get.

VOICE OF NORTH. Are we going?

> *The voice seems to come from somewhere else.* ANNIE *spins round with the torch to reveal a child (or very lifelike mannequin) standing on the other side of the room.*

ANNIE. That was… fast. Good girl. Come on.

VOICE OF NORTH. Shall we go get Mommy?

ANNIE. No. Mummy's being crazy, baby. We're gonna – she's gonna come join us when she's better.

VOICE OF NORTH. Can I see her?

ANNIE. No. Not now. Just trust me okay?

VOICE OF NORTH. Okay, Daddy.

ANNIE. Get in the car now. Do your seatbelt up.

VOICE OF NORTH. Okay, Daddy.

ANNIE. Good girl. You're a superstar, baby.

VOICE OF NORTH. Daddy?

ANNIE. Yeah?

VOICE OF NORTH. Just breathe okay?

ANNIE. Sorry, baby.

VOICE OF NORTH. It's okay.

ANNIE. I'll breathe.

VOICE OF NORTH. Can I give you a hug? Before we go?

ANNIE. Yeah, of course.

I'm sorry, baby.

I just wanna help. I'm just trying / to

VOICE OF NORTH. Breathe.

ANNIE. Okay, baby.

North. You know when I died. Before I came back.

VOICE OF NORTH. Yes, Daddy.

ANNIE. How did it feel?

VOICE OF NORTH. It felt sad. But I didn't really know what was going on.

Silence.

Daddy?

ANNIE. Yeah?

VOICE OF NORTH. Can I sing you a song? One of yours?

ANNIE. Of course you can.

Of course you can.

Go on.

VOICE OF NORTH. Will you listen?

ANNIE. Yes.

Pause.

VOICE OF NORTH. I'm nervous.

ANNIE. Don't be nervous. Never be nervous.

Pause.

VOICE OF NORTH. Okay.

Pause.

Sound of North singing 'I'll Fly Away'.

ANNIE *goes to clap.*

She stops herself.

What did you think Daddy?

She doesn't clap.

Daddy?

She doesn't clap.

Was it good?

Do you think I'm a good singer?

Do you think I'm gonna be great someday?

She doesn't clap.

She doesn't clap.

Blackout.

You don't look like my daddy.

The End.

A Nick Hern Book

Kanye The First first published in Great Britain in 2017 as a paperback original by Nick Hern Books Limited, The Glasshouse, 49a Goldhawk Road, London W12 8QP, in association with HighTide and Paul Jellis

Cover image: Luke W. Robson / lococreative.com

Designed and typeset by Nick Hern Books, London
Printed in the UK by Mimeo Ltd, Huntingdon, Cambridgeshire PE29 6XX

A CIP catalogue record for this book is available from the British Library

ISBN 978 1 84842 689 4